Who's Crazy Anyway

Who's Crazy Anyway

Everything You Always Wanted to Know About
the Risks and Benefits of Psychotherapy
But Didn't Want to Have to Pay a
Therapist to Find Out

by

Joan Mazza M.S. LMHC
Psychotherapist • Speaker • Author • Seminar Leader

toExcel
San Jose New York Lincoln Shanghai

Who's Crazy Anyway

Published by toExcel
an imprint of iUniverse.com, Inc.

For information address:
iUniverse.com, Inc.
620 North 48th Street
Suite 201
Lincoln, NE 68504-3467
www.iuniverse.com

ISBN: 0-595-00230-7

Printed in the United States of America

For Dianne Grandstrom
who caught this book
at the moment of its birth

Acknowledgements

Many thanks to my friends, teachers, and colleagues who discussed with me and contributed to the concepts in this book: John Bradshaw, Dale Buchanan, Heidi Boehringer, Nina Garcia, Joyce Gilbert, Virginia Havens, Lesley Kleiner, Joan Lindsay, Linda Newman, Poldi Orlando, Bill Rea, Rosemarie Uman, Noreen Wald, and Len Worley.

Much gratitude to those who read the complete manuscript and offered their suggestions: Norma Berkman, Dianne Grandstrom, Lana Schulman, and Joyce Sweeney.

Contents

Who's Crazy anyway?
Everything You Always Wanted To Know About
The Risks And Benefits Of Psychotherapy
But Didn't Want To have To Pay A Therapist To Find Out

1. Preface: my ax to grind

No book is written in a vacuum. When a person decides to write a book and to devote so much time to such a complex and demanding endeavor, you can be certain the author brings herself into the material every time. Even when writing fiction, the subject matter and the characters call to the author from the depths of the psyche. This book is no different.

When I started seeing a psychiatrist, I was unhappily married and wanted things to change. Like most people, I entered therapy with the hope of finding happiness and a more satisfying way to live. I believed therapy would help me find the courage and confidence to leave my marriage.

Much of the therapy I received was helpful and educational, especially in the early years. Later, what happened seemed more abusive than helpful or instructive. In many ways, my psychiatrist reinforced and exacerbated the very wounds I'd come to therapy to heal: feeling oppressed and dominated by my parents and later by my husband, feeling imprisoned and unable to express my talents and intelligence, feeling restricted by society for being female. This is a perfect example of what Alice Miller describes in her books: how the therapy itself can re-wound the client who comes to therapy to resolve and overcome the legacy of his upbringing.

While saying he was "helping" me, my therapist was also exploiting me personally by asking for favors, keeping me isolated from others, focusing only on the negative aspects of my character, giving advice and direction, and having more and more influence in every area of my life. He violated nearly all of the rules of ethical, professional standards in mental health, especially those concerning dual relationships, which refers to having a professional and social relationship with a client/patient.

Whenever I wanted to leave the therapy, he insisted I wasn't ready. Each time, he told me I was being resistant to the issues we were working on. We concentrated on my shortcomings, defects, and mistakes. Whatever I did, including following his advice, was labeled neurotic. He forbade me to talk to anyone else about my problems or about what was happening in my therapy with him. He also didn't want me talking to others about my social contacts with him and his family.

After sixteen years, it was clear that I was never going to be ready to leave if I waited for him to make the decision. I had become too big a contributor to his regular income; I was the personal ally he needed to bolster his fragile ego. After severing my ties with him and his family, I began to see how much damage he'd done, rivaling any of my hurts from my family of origin or past relationships. I began to see how his treatment of me had resembled that of a cult leader; he had used nearly every one of their strategies of mind control. I had refused to see his need for power or my contribution to giving away my personal autonomy.

In the years since, I have considered bringing a lawsuit against him. Several of my professional colleagues urged me to do so. But I decided that long court proceedings and dredging up my bad feelings would help me less than getting on with my life and warning others of the possible dangers of therapy. With hindsight, it seems as if the best evidence for my being "crazy" was having stayed in therapy for so long with someone who was no longer helpful.

Who's Crazy, Anyway? is not the story of my personal experience as a patient in therapy, but it is certainly colored by that experience. I have chosen to take what I learned during my therapy and then later in my training and studies to help others make more informed decisions than I did. The energy in the anger and outrage from my experience has helped to fuel the motivation to write this book. If that means I have "an ax to grind," then I acknowledge that.

Having "an ax to grind" usually means having a selfish motive. I recognize that part of the purpose of this book is to heal my own wounds. I hope that it will also benefit others while it puts an end to my feeling like I was a victim of an unscrupulous and dangerous therapist.

People who know me and my work today find it hard to believe that I could have allowed myself to be so manipulated and controlled by someone else. They have said that if this could happen to me—a relatively bright and educated woman whom most people don't see as either compliant or passive, then it could happen to anyone.

For that reason, I hope what I have to say will help others to avoid some of the pitfalls of psychotherapy, while also explaining some of the techniques of therapy and what they can expect.

I believe that psychotherapy has a lot to offer people in distress when it is practiced responsibly, ethically, and with caution. By becoming more self-aware, patient with yourself and others, better able to manage your life and your emotions, you can have more happiness and move toward realizing your potential.

2. How to use this book

This book is written in "sound bytes." Each topic has a brief explanation and, in some cases, examples. It was written to be read in order. However, you can start anywhere and use this book in the best way that works for you.

It is impossible to list all the therapy models and techniques available today in the mental health professions. New concepts and techniques are being developed by pioneering and innovative therapists all the time. I have tried to cover the main schools of thought and practice, including some of those that might be considered by more traditional therapists to be "on the fringe."

The extensive bibliography offers books for study in those areas where you might want to have more information. In some cases, authors are listed in the text so that you can refer to their books in the bibliography. By no means, do I claim to cover every possible diagnosis, distressing mental state, and solution to emotional problems. For the most part, this is a book to encourage you to think critically about your own problems and how you can resolve them. It suggests, in many ways, that you carefully choose what type of help to pursue, and then be willing to evaluate that help as you proceed. It also suggests questions to ask yourself and questions to ask your therapist. You know what's best for you, even if you feel unsure as you begin.

3. Why do you want to begin psychotherapy?

People usually enter psychotherapy at times when they are in emotional or psychological pain. They may have felt unhappy, anxious, fearful, or dissatisfied with their lives for some time and hope that seeing a professional will give them some relief and comfort. Perhaps they've experienced symptoms such as phobias or panic attacks; perhaps they want to deal with the problems caused by what they suspect is as an addiction or an eating disorder. Their relationships may be less gratifying than they would like; they seem to be on a self-destructive path. Job problems and financial worries sometimes cause people to feel overwhelmed and hopeless.

People who come to therapy often feel as if their lives are not working the way they want them to and may feel as if they've tried everything they can think of. Therapy is their last hope.

Another way that people come to therapy is when they have been referred by someone else. Maybe a mate or lover has said that going to therapy is a requirement of continuing the relationship.

In general, people in these states have come to doubt their own judgments and perceptions. They are confused and distressed. Sometimes, they feel paralyzed or their lives seem to be spinning out of control. They may feel incompetent, helpless, and hopeless.

So they come to a therapist with the hope of getting some answers and direction to the same problems all of us have in being human: finding love and purpose, feeling worthwhile and accepted, being at peace with ourselves and others, having meaning and pleasure in our lives. They want comfort, reassurance, and perhaps validation of their perceptions and impressions.

But their state of mind at the time of making contact may be putting them at their biggest risk when entering therapy. By admitting they are confused and doubting their ability to make good decisions, they are prone to take whatever the therapist says as The Truth and not ask the questions they should be asking before embarking on such an intense and intimate journey.

Stephen Wolinsky, author of *Trances People Live*, suggests that people are *already in trance* when they come to therapy. The task of therapy is to break the trance so that the individual can begin to think more clearly and make decisions more consciously. When people come to therapy, they are open and suggestible. Because they may be malleable or desperate, without their critical thinking operating, they are apt to be gullible and not as discriminating as they should be when choosing a therapist. This makes them easy prey for untrained and unqualified counselors who may be working outside the usual standards of care and training in mental health. Sometimes those therapists promise "instant transformation" or other unrealistic outcomes of their techniques.

In many ways, the individual who is considering therapy is caught in a Catch-22. It's important to ask questions, to know what you need and can expect from a therapist, to be assertive about setting therapy goals and boundaries, to be realistic about the limits of what therapy can do. But if you were this clear, confident, and able to express your needs, feelings, and thoughts about therapy, you probably wouldn't need it.

Still, a person in distress and seeking help can benefit from having extra information while approaching this important decision. After all, when you enter psychotherapy, you are putting your trust in a complete stranger, telling the most secret and embarrassing details of your life, opening yourself up to the scrutiny of another. For some, this is their first experience with intimacy. But because the therapy encounter is structured so that only the client or patient reveals himself extensively, the interaction is not real intimacy but an uneven intimacy. By definition, the relationship is unequal. It is asymmetrical. The focus is only on the client's concerns. This may feed a certain narcissism and childlike need to be the center of attention—which can feel good. However, it can also cloud the client's ability to assess the benefits and progress of the therapy. Many of the topics that follow will help you to avoid that Catch-22.

4. What is the problem? How serious is it? Is this an area of discomfort you've been aware of for some time? Or is it something brought to your attention by others?

Before seeking a professional, ask yourself what have you done on your own to try to solve the problem. Have you examined your role in the cause of the problem? If this is a conflict with another person, have you approached the individual and expressed your desire to improve the relationship? If you are feeling unsuccessful or stuck, what have you done in the past to get unstuck? You might consider taking some time out now to write out what your problem is and what you've done so far to try to solve it.

Recall the times when you have solved a problem or succeeded at something. Notice what resources and inner strengths you drew upon to accomplish your success. How might those strengths and talents be used this time to improve your situation on your own? If you feel powerful or competent in one area of your life, consider using that memory and those abilities in this other problematic area.

If your area of concern is one that has been brought to your attention by others, only you can decide whether it is something you want to address in therapy or on your own. People close to you might be complaining about your behavior, the way you respond or not, your attitude or general demeanor, what they might call your insensitivity or lack of awareness. They might object to your habits. Perhaps they tell you that you have an addiction or an obsession that's driving them crazy and they want you to get help.

However, any changes you make in yourself or in your awareness and thinking have to be *your choice* to make. They, like you, can only change themselves and it's not up to other people to fix you. They can say what bothers them or how your behavior affects your relationship with them, but you are the only one who can decide to change you. If they feel your behavior (such as managing your anger or drinking) affects how they feel about you or your ability to be in relationship with them, you might want to consider whether they have a valid concern. Maybe a closer look at yourself and how you affect others can be helpful to you and make your life more enjoyable. Perhaps you can learn from what they have to say. It's always good to listen respectfully to another point of view and honestly examine what others offer. We often have blind spots about ourselves that others can see.

At the same time, others may object to your growth, independence, and increased success because it changes the balance of power and influence in the relationship. Frequently, when a person who has been passive and submissive in a relationship begins to show some assertiveness, make requests, or speak openly, close associates object. They may say, "You've changed!" Their tone indicates they like you less or that they disapprove of the changes you've made. Their reactions might discourage you from continuing to evolve the way you need to. It may cast doubt on your desire to live in a way that is more true to your authentic self.

Weighing a criticism against your own perceptions is always tricky. You may wonder if their criticism highlights one of your blind spots or if they are just trying to get you back into the old patterns that worked better *for them*. After all, if you're passive and docile they get *their* needs met.

At such times, it's helpful to have *several* trusted friends whom you can ask for honest feedback. Later in this book, we'll look at building a support network.

5. Is this an issue for psychotherapy or can I weather the storm on my own and let time heal? Is the problem simply part of the normal ups and downs of living?

Most life problems are not so serious that they need professional intervention. Life gives all of us difficulties or stresses that will pass and change in time. Examples might include the emotions you have during final exams in school, while looking after a newborn child, caring for an elderly or sick parent, going through a divorce, experiencing a big disappointment or the loss of a loved one.

While it may be helpful for you to have a sounding board to express your feelings and hear how others have handled comparable predicaments, it may not be necessary for you to have professional assistance. Talking with a trusted friend or family member can relieve the pent-up feelings. Try telling yourself, "This too shall pass," and see how your mind responds. If the problems you perceive seem overwhelming to you or if you are in great distress, a few sessions with a professional can be helpful—even if similar problems may not seem overwhelming to others. Some coaching in your coping skills might be all you need.

Many problems such as the ones mentioned above are part of normal living. Being a mentally and emotionally healthy person doesn't mean that you always feel wonderful or never feel like your life is out of control. Having it together doesn't mean that life is bliss all the time.

But if feeling that your life is out of control is your usual state, if your problems are giving you intense suffering and pain, then you might want to consider seeing a therapist. A little bit of competent psychotherapy can go a long way.

6. Diagnosing yourself; evaluating your symptoms.

It would be helpful for you to make an effort to diagnose or assess your concerns before you make an appointment. The more clear you are about your problem, the more likely you are to find or be referred to someone who can help you.

What is the specific nature of the problem? Mental health professionals classify mental and emotional distress into several categories, including:

a. moods and emotions, including extreme highs and lows such as mania and depression, suicidal feelings, an inability to manage one's anger or grief.

b. anxiety and panic attacks, unrealistic fears—also called phobias, or an inability to interact with others or have satisfying relationships out of extreme shyness or nervousness around other people.

c. thoughts and perceptions, also called cognitive disorders, which include confusion or an inability to think clearly,having trouble staying focused on a train of thought, or being unable to solve ordinary problems by thinking them through and taking the proper action.

d. impulsiveness or poor impulse control and making bad choices such as gambling or setting fires; obsessions such as repetitive and intrusive thoughts and compulsions such as frequent hand-washing. Such people might say they can't control their behavior. With the right treatment, they can improve their degree of control and expand the range of control they already have but are unaware of.

e. eating disorders such as bulimia (eating large quantities and then purging by vomiting and using laxatives), anorexia (starving yourself), over-eating and health concerns related to obesity.

f. sleep disorders such as insomnia (the inability to fall asleep or stay asleep) and falling asleep when you want to be awake (narcolepsy), night terrors, nightmares, and sleep walking.

g.   substance-related disorders such as addictions to drugs (both prescription and illegal drugs such as marijuana, cocaine, heroine), alcohol, nicotine, and caffeine.

h.   relationship problems with a spouse, child, or others.

i.   sexual problems and dysfunctions such as an inability to be aroused or to reach orgasm. Some sexual disorders include having a sexual interest that is against the law (such as a sexual preference for children or publicly exposing your genitals). Other sexual concerns might be fears or embarrassment about sexual matters in general. Some sexual problems are not psychologically based, but are caused by physical and physiological processes from aging or diseases such as diabetes.

j.   dissociative disorders and attentional disorders such as feeling disconnected from yourself and the world or frequently feeling spaced-out or disconnected from reality.

k.   psychotic disorders including schizophrenia, which might involve hallucinations such as seeing or hearing things that are not present; or delusions, such as believing you are being poisoned or followed when you are not.

l.   spiritual sickness—feeling that life has no meaning or purpose, a kind of aimlessness and dissatisfaction with life circumstances, or unnamed distress.

This last category is sometimes referred to a an existential problem and is a normal part of coming to terms with one's life. However, some people seek guidance or support during intensely emotional times.

These very brief descriptions are not all of the categories in the Diagnostic and Statistical Manual of Mental Disorders, Fourth Edition (DSM-IV). DSM also includes other disorders such as personality disorders (paranoid, narcissistic, antisocial, etc). How these labels are accepted or not by others would certainly vary depending on your culture and the era in which you live. A Victorian woman would think women of today were mentally unbalanced to dress or talk the way they do. We might assess a Victorian woman as uptight, narrow-minded, racist, and self-punishing. While it may be considered appropriate to express feelings or speak your mind in one ethnic or cultural group, the same behavior might be considered "insane" or at least grossly rude in another. The acceptance and meaning of tattoos, body-piercing and painting, and certain kinds of clothing will vary widely depending on the beliefs of an ethnic, religious, or cultural group.

Paula Caplan, in *They Say You're Crazy: The Inside Story of the DSM,* shows us how the DSM is assembled. What is determined to be a mental illness may be a somewhat arbitrary decision, depending who is on the committee and what is of public interest at the time.

These situational values remind us that ***mental illness is always culturally defined.*** Someone else might think you're crazy because the most important aspect in your life is your art or your spirituality. That is less your concern than what *you* believe to be a problem. Your assessment is what counts the most.

It is also possible for you to consider something a problem and your therapist to reassure you that it is not a problem unless you make it one. However, your therapist might also define something as a problem when you don't. It is up to you to decide what you want to address in therapy.

7. Symptoms as messages from the unconscious

One way that can be helpful to look at symptoms and problems is to understand them as messages. If you are feeling depressed or irritable, this is information that something in your life needs to change. When our fingers burn, we react quickly. The pain is a signal to take them out of the flame to protect ourselves from further injury. When we hurt in other ways by being tormented by intrusive thoughts, uncomfortable emotions, or physical aches and pains that don't seem to have an explanation, we can ask ourselves how these are indications of something that needs to be examined further for change. What are our bodies telling us?

If I have a sudden stomach ache, I might ask what just happened that feels tough to digest, or hard to swallow, or difficult to assimilate. If my head hurts, I might consider whether there is something I don't want to think about or face and the pain distracts me. If I use drugs or alcohol, what is it that I need to anesthetize myself against? What anxiety am I trying to drown?

Any behavior we consider undesirable, even complex and tenacious behaviors like drinking excessively, often provide the person with satisfactions they don't want to give up. What is the positive side of this negative behavior? For some, drinking is a way to retreat from the pain of living in the world. For others, drinking provides an opportunity to socialize, to "let their hair down" or loosen up in ways they cannot allow themselves when sober. Also, they enjoy the rituals of alcohol consumption, which might include giving themselves a transition period after work, toasting each other, and celebrating important events.

Similarly, in families, the problem child's behavior might serve the purpose of creating crises to keep the parents together. The parents worry about this child rather than focusing on the problems of their relationship. In their concern, they will stay together. The "symptom" has an intent that may not be conscious, but serves the participants well. When these needs are made conscious and are satisfied in other ways, the child's undesirable behavior can change.

8. Addiction

The term addiction has become part of our everyday vocabulary. People are quick to say they have an addiction when they feel passionate about some hobby or some new interest. Because they enjoy an activity and they look forward to doing it, they might say they are addicted. It may be dancing, collecting things, making love, or going to the movies. To qualify as an addiction, the behavior has to be a problem for the person who is engaging in it.

What makes a true addiction is that the practice is used to stay out of touch with your true feelings. You use the behavior to numb awareness or consciousness and these actions result in negative consequences in your life.

If you feel you cannot control what you do, have to lie about it, if your behavior would cause serious problems in your work or personal life if the behavior were made public, if you are consumed with thoughts of this activity so that other areas of your life are in jeopardy (such as jobs or relationships) because you are not meeting your responsibilities, then the behavior might qualify as an addiction. If you are ashamed of the behavior or unable to stop yourself when you want to, then this might be something you want to talk about with a mental health professional. Exceptions to calling the behavior an addiction include the fear of someone finding out you are gay if that would result in your losing your housing or employment. Some political beliefs might put a person in jeopardy, so lying may be prudent rather than a sign of shame or addition.

9. Sexual addiction or celebrating sexuality?

In the language of addiction and recovery, people have begun to talk about having sexual addictions. An interest in sex, especially when a person has a fair share of their attention and focus devoted to sex, is sometimes considered evidence of an "addiction." The behaviors associated with this interest are seen as evidence of a "disease," which needs to be treated. Of course, this trend is common throughout the psychotherapeutic industry, making many behaviors into diseases that need treatment and medication. The profit motive cannot be ignored when we examine any newly discovered problem and treatment centers open to "cure" the people who suffer from them. (For more on this discussion, see *Diseasing of America* by Stanton Peele.)

Is it possible to be enthusiastic about sexuality, to celebrate sexuality and sensuality without being addicted? How do you know when your interest is more than healthy passion and pleasure and has become a problem?

Usually, you know when some behavior or thought pattern has become a problem because you are in distress about it. You want to stop the behavior and can't. You may feel you can't control yourself and you are compelled to do things you believe are immoral or harmful. This is a judgment call of the person who is involved in the behavior. When someone else tells you that you have a sexual addiction because you enjoy erotic literature and sexually explicit films, what they are saying is that this would be a problem for them. Is it a problem for you? Do you want to stop? Do you feel driven to have one love affair after another and you can't seem to stop yourself? Do you have to lie about it? Do you make excuses for your behavior that feel false to you? In what way is your behavior a problem? Who is complaining about it? Does it affect your romantic partner or spouse? Are you violating a monogamous agreement that you made with your partner?

The danger of labeling any behavior a "disease" is that it implies there is some outside force like an infectious agent, that is the cause of the behavior. The disease label may then be used, as it has been in the courts, to defend misbehavior and to diminish the responsibility of the individual. When loss of control becomes an excuse for misbehavior, we may be going down a slippery slope that infantilizes people instead of encouraging them to act as adults responsible for their behavior and choices.

If you feel shame and remorse over your style of sexuality or the frequency of your sexual contacts, you may wonder if you have a sexual addiction. You might also want to talk about it if you frequently use sex to fill an inner emptiness, rather than finding other sources of love, power, and self-esteem. If you are concerned that your sexual behavior is misbehavior because of your choice of partners (underage or otherwise inappropriate choices) or because your behavior feels driven and excessive, you may want to discuss these emotions with a professional.

Clearly, the social norms of your culture and era will influence whether a behavior is judged "normal" or "not normal." Make sure you participate in determining what is normal for you.

10. Codependency

Another psychological term that has made its way into popular speech is *codependent*. As with many overused words, its original meaning has gotten somewhat lost. Codependency does not mean being bonded, in love, or attached to others. The term is used to describe people who are more involved with the lives of others than they are in their own lives. They constantly worry, interfere, give guidance, and advice to others who do not necessarily seek out this attention. In psychological language, we might say these people become so enmeshed with others that they have poor boundaries. They don't know where they leave off and other people begin. They think more about others and what is happening in the lives of others than about their own lives. They may complain that what their mates or children do reflects on them. Some can feel worthwhile only by being around others who shine, basking in their glory.

Frequently, they need to surround themselves with others who can prop them up with symbols of wealth or high status such as expensive cars, jewelry, and clothing. Codependents are the people who are likely to emphasize relationship to the exclusion of other aspects of life. They may feel their lives are over or become suicidal when a lover breaks off the relationship. They are easily slighted and offended and manage their emotional reactions poorly.

Many of these patterns of behavior can be effectively improved by education and skill training. Applying the disease model for unhappy relationship patterns may not be as helpful as building skills in communication, self-awareness, and emotional intelligence.

Healthy relationships are made of whole people who can live separately, but choose to be *interdependent* to share their resources and support each other.

If a therapist tells you that you are codependent, ask for more information about this assessment. What does it mean for your treatment or therapy goals?

11. Depression. Is it a time to go inward and reflect?

There are many times in our life when we question how we are spending our time, what relationships we are investing in, what value our work has. Our lives include periods when we feel down, with little energy or enthusiasm. We may wonder why we're here or why we should continue on our present paths. Our daily activities may seem pointless or a waste of time.

These may be normal times of self-reflection. These intervals may be uncomfortable and we may be inclined to call them depression, but they are frequently part of the normal cycles of mood and self-awareness. If you are continuing in your daily business, able to work, interact with others, and meet your daily responsibilities, I would suggest you consider thinking about these low times in words other than "depression."

Perhaps this is a time you need to withdraw from the world a little and rethink your priorities and choices. At other times in history, people regularly took time out of their daily routines to go on retreat. They might have taken three days to be alone in a natural setting with time to think and experience themselves quietly. Or they might have joined with others in silent companionship to pray. They used these times to contemplate their purpose and place in the universe and to be more connected to themselves.

Retreats were a socially acceptable form of behavior and no one accused participants of isolating themselves or becoming hermits. For a few days each year, they could go into a self-chosen form of hibernation, away from the daily stresses and routines.

Our busy lives today don't often allow us to take these times. We might have to tell ourselves this is a professional workshop in order to allow ourselves to spend the time and money. Yet we still need these times to withdraw, go inward, and give ourselves a chance to regroup, restore ourselves, and recharge our batteries. When we don't take this time consciously, our bodies and minds might rebel with illnesses that force us into hibernation. Worse, we might experience what we call a "breakdown" so we will be hospitalized and justify our withdrawal from the world.

If you're feeling down, ask yourself what you need. Time alone? Time away? Time to be with others where you can open yourself and share your personal truths? Take this time, if only a few hours now and then. Schedule a time when you can withdraw and just think or daydream and let go of your daily cares.

On the other hand, depression can be very serious. If you find yourself thinking that life isn't worth living, that you are feeling unable to go on, or are feeling helpless and hopeless most of the time, then you should seek professional help. *If you have fre-quent thoughts of harming yourself or killing yourself (or some-one else) or have made a plan to do so, get help immediately, even if you have to go to a hospital emergency room.* Death is not a solution. Ask yourself how you imagine your death will affect others. What makes death seem to be a solution? How else might you accomplish what the idea of death seems to do for you? How else might you alleviate the pain you are experiencing? Get help to discuss these thoughts.

Give yourself the opportunity to see your present situation from another point of view. The problems that seem over-whelming and frightening to you now will appear very different in a few days and certainly in a few months and years. The prob-lems you had years ago were likely resolved by your increased maturity or changes in your life circumstances. Some of them might seem laughable to you now.

Nothing stays the same. Everything changes. Problems often get resolved simply by the passage of time.

Sometimes the problem doesn't change, but your ability to deal with it changes or you change your perspective and no longer see it as a problem. You have had tough times before and each time they seemed like the worst times, yet you managed to handle your situation. You have resources within you that you may not even be aware of to resolve your own predicaments. Therapy is one way to tap into those resources and gain the skills and abilities to handle what life presents you.

12. Learned Optimism

Martin Seligman, in his book, *Learned Optimism*, shows us how the three Ps of pessimism contribute to feelings of depression. People who are prone to depression are likely to have habits of viewing the bad things that happen to them as pervasive, permanent, and personal. When something bad happens, they tell themselves, "It's always like this [permanent]; I can never do anything right [pervasive]; and it's all my fault because I'm a loser [personal]."

These people then ruminate on these negative thoughts, finding "evidence" in their lives and expecting more catastrophes. With help in therapy, these people can become aware of these patterns and learn to dispute the negative thoughts: "I'm not a loser; I have a good job and I do it competently. Sometimes bad things happen, but I have good things in my life, too. This is temporary; this will pass. Everybody feels crummy sometimes."

Changing your thinking patterns to a more optimistic style can be effective in stopping the negative thought cascade that can lead to deep depression. Optimistic people are more likely to see problems as temporary, limited to the specific instance, and often due to outside causes beyond their control.

This is a sample of a cognitive approach to mood disorders. Later, we'll examine other cognitive methods in psychotherapy.

13. Is the problem inside you or outside you?

Some people enter therapy with the belief that their problems are outside of them. Other people are making them feel bad, telling them what to do, causing their problems, and controlling their lives. Their boss is cruel or unreasonable; their mate is cold and indifferent; their children won't do what they are told.

These people come to therapy with the idea that they will learn how to get other people to do what they want them to do. What they often find out is that the problem is usually inside the person who states the problem. If you are unhappy with your circumstances, you have the power to change the circumstances or to change the way you see them. You can change your context or you can change your interpretation (the meaning) of what you are calling a problem.

In short, you can only change yourself, not others. People often forget this or see it as some truism that ironically doesn't apply to them. Maybe you need to change your perspective or attitude. Or maybe you need to change your situation by looking for another job or place to live. Maybe the way you relate to others needs to be different—more patient, compassionate, or assertive.

What is interesting about doing inner work through psychotherapy is that when the person who comes to therapy changes by acting differently with others, the other people around also change. You might think of your situation as being in balance (though not in a positive way) as it is now. All the people in your circle interact with you according to well-established patterns of behavior. These are part of our daily habits. If you change, their responses might also change and your circumstances will therefore change as well. What can you do that will be different and helpful? This is one that the changes you make in yourself will make positive changes in your life.

14. The benefits of therapy and inner work

Many people fear finding out about themselves. They fear looking inside themselves and knowing what true feelings and desires might be lurking in the darkest corners of their psyches. The fear keeps them from learning about themselves. What may be worse, the effort they make to keep these parts hidden saps them of energy that could be used to live more joyfully and with more satisfaction. The chronic exhaustion that many people experience is due to this stuffing down of feelings and fear of knowing their true selves. Ironically, they also stuff down their best talents and assets—what they would be most proud of if they allowed themselves to blossom as they were meant to.

Inner work brings us self-awareness. We begin to see ourselves as part of the human community. We are able to interact with others with conscious awareness of our expectations and demands. We reduce our rules for ourselves and others to be perfect. We become aware of how others might perceive us. Slowly, we stop warring with ourselves and others.

By doing this inner work—in or outside of psychotherapy—our choices expand and our lives improve. We may experience the loss of innocence around our ideal image of ourselves and others, but we also flower in a way that may have been undreamed of before doing this work of self-exploration.

15. What is mental health? What is normal?

These are two different questions, but many people see them as one. What is "normal" is what is average in any population. Normal may also be those traits, behaviors, and reactions that are expected or occur most frequently and are considered acceptable. That doesn't mean they are mentally healthy or even desirable. What is normal in one culture may be considered abnormal or crazy in another. Boisterous laughter in a public place might be acceptable in New York but considered abnormal in a pub in England.

What does mental health mean to you? And how would you know if you or someone else had it? What would you observe? You might want to answer these in your own mind before continuing. Make a list of what you think constitutes mental health.

Some of the criteria for mental health might include having the ability to access a variety of choices; greater flexibility, emotional control, clarity, serenity, peace, happiness; intimate and respectful relationships; self-confidence and self-awareness; ability to take risks and live with ambiguity; acceptance of your own humanity and imperfections; trust in and expressing your feelings; being personally responsible for your actions, personal health, and well being; living with integrity; having a life that's balanced and shows moderation rather than extremes; being able to ask for what you want and need; being able to defend your rights; having skills to cope with life's stressors; having persistence, tenacity, and follow-through; doing work you enjoy; realizing your potential; enjoying lifelong learning; using your talents and creativity; being self-disciplined; seeing life realistically; having empathy and compassion for others; and sharing yourself with others for mutual benefit.

Unfortunately, these descriptions do not apply to many of the general or average population. So, ask yourself if you want to be healthy or if you only want to be "normal."

16. When you want to persuade someone else to go to therapy

Perhaps you have purchased this book with the thought to give it to someone else because you think he or she needs therapy. You might have a mate or friend or family member who is suffering and could use some introspective work. Perhaps this person is driving you crazy and you want to see him "get fixed" so he won't be unreasonable or irrational.

When the people we love or those we must interact with daily are difficult, we want them to change. We are inclined to focus on their faults and how they could be different so our lives would be easier. If only they would understand how they are making themselves and everybody else miserable, then things would be better.

People often do come to therapy because someone else suggests it. It's quite common for a spouse to insist that their mate attend some sessions together when the relationship or family is in crisis. This is often helpful for everyone, including those family members who don't go themselves. If you are the one who sees the problem, you can start by working on yourself rather than trying to begin by sending the other person to "get fixed." Perhaps you are putting your own problems onto others or objecting to their growth because it interferes with what you want for yourself.

Questions to ask yourself when you want someone else to go to therapy

1.   How am I contributing to this problem?
2.   What do I do when I interact with this person that creates the problem or makes the problem worse?

3. How am I being critical and negative?
4. What can I do differently?
5. What do I need from this person?
6. How can I help?
7. Can I give to this person what I need for myself?
8. Can I love this person just as he/she is?
9. What can I do and say that will support this person's growth?
10. How is this person showing me my own faults and defects of character?
11. Is there some other way to see this person or some other way to interpret this person's behavior?
12. What do I want therapy to do for this person?
13. What changes am I expecting or hoping for?
14. Can I ask for these changes directly and without anger or threats?
15. What experiences in my past are contributing to my distress with this person?

If you still want to suggest therapy as a possible help to another, you might consider presenting the idea of psychotherapy as a process where people learn about themselves, improve their skills for dealing with life's problems, and gain greater self-awareness and self-confidence.

Unfortunately, you can only change yourself. However, when you change your own attitude and your own behavior *the way you want the other person to change*, frequently everything else begins to improve.

17. The impact of your therapy on your relationships

When you begin your own therapy, you can expect others to react. Some people will be pleased and others dismayed or frightened. As you make changes, your relationships will change because you will behave differently with others. As discussed above, some of this impact will be positive. On the other hand, the people you are closest to may feel threatened by your entering therapy or counseling. They may worry that you are complaining about them, making them look bad, telling only your side of the story and not treating them fairly. They may fear you will disclose confidential information about them and see this as a breach of the privacy and intimacy you shared with them. For a mate or a spouse, this can feel like betrayal or infidelity. Your partner might become angry or withdrawn, feeling abandoned and left out of the therapy.

It is important that you accept these reactions with compassion and understanding, especially if these are relationships you wish to maintain. If these relationships are the focus of your therapy, then you might consider sharing your intent to have the relationship continue. Let your partner know that's why you want to talk about it. Say that you are willing to look at what you can do to improve the quality of the relationship and you value it enough to get professional help to do it. Reassurance is appropriate.

Certainly, your mate or partner might want to have a joint session with you to air his/her point of view. This should be viewed a welcome option so that the therapy process isn't cloaked in mystery and secrecy, which might make him/her fearful. A competent therapist will be willing to meet anyone you would like to bring to therapy because it can be helpful to your work in therapy for the therapist to meet others who are important to you. Sometimes, having one or a few sessions together can help to defuse the potentially explosive reaction of a mate who views therapy as going outside of the relationship.

On the other hand, if your mate or someone else is actively discouraging you from going to therapy, you can ask directly what their objections are without speculating on what their motives might be. "What are your concerns?" "Why do you think this is a mistake?" Listen carefully to what they have to say and try to understand the wariness expressed. Is it reasonable? Do they need further reassurance or are the concerns well founded? Throughout this book, we consider many of the concerns that people should think about before entering therapy.

However, if anyone you know tells you s/he will terminate the relationship with you if you continue in therapy, then this is a good time to take a look at how this person is attempting to control your life and personal decision-making. The choice to go or not go to psychotherapy should be yours to make as an adult in charge of your own life. Threats or ultimata from another may be an excellent time to reevaluate your relationship with this person. It may be an opportunity to take your first step into autonomy by letting the other person know this decision is yours to make. This person can express their distress and concerns and you can listen respectfully, but allowing another to make this decision for you is giving up your freedom and can only lead to more control and a shrinking of your life choices.

18. What are your goals and expectations?

In coming to therapy, you probably have some complaints and/or symptoms that you would like to talk about. If you've gone over the possible problems people bring to therapy that were listed earlier, you may have an idea of what you want to work on.

If you go to therapy with the idea that you want more happiness or to have a better life, you would probably do well to be more specific and choose some particular goals for your therapy. Good therapists will ask you what you want to accomplish and what your goals are. If your goals are vague and undefined, how will you know if you accomplished them?

What might others notice about you when you accomplish your therapy goals?

When setting goals in therapy or in any other aspect of your life, consider designing your goals to be SMART:
- Specific
- Measurable
- Action-oriented or Active
- Reasonable
- Time-oriented

A smart goal is *specific* rather than vague. I can say that I want to be a better student. What is better? What do I mean by student? Better grades in school? More time spent studying? More attentive in class? A wider range of knowledge in related subjects?

The goal is *measurable.* It can be quantified. I will know I am more responsible when I get to work on time every day rather than late. Or I will study a minimum of one hour a day without any interruptions.

The goal is *active or action-oriented.* Feeling better is what we would all like, but what are we doing to feel better? The goal is an activity, something that you have control over by how you behave or think. To get along better with others (a vague goal), I might say that I will listen when others speak and ask them a question to clarify what they are saying and to show my interest in them personally.

The goal must be *reasonable.* If I'm not exercising at all, to say that my exercise program will be two hours four times a week may not be reasonable to accomplish at first. It's too much of a dramatic change from my present state of inactivity. Starting with a fifteen-minute walk three days a week is more manageable.

You are not likely to write a book in the next three months if you've never written at all, but promising to write three or four pages a week is do-able. You are more likely to do it because the goal is not overwhelming. *Nothing breeds success like a little success.* If your goals are too high or too ambitious, you are likely to give up early or feel like a failure. Set reachable, reasonable goals and you can raise your aspirations as you achieve them.

The goals should be *time-oriented.* I'm going to talk more to my mate is a worthy goal, but how much is "more?" I can say that I will set aside time after dinner for the next month to stay in conversation. For the next month, rather than jumping up to clean up or to do other things after dinner, I'll sit at the table for ten extra minutes. This is measurable and time-oriented. You may want to set your goals for a week, month, or a year. "Some day" is the opposite of time-oriented goals.

Choose one, SMART goal now for your therapy and see if it meets these five criteria. How can you state it more clearly to make it SMART?

If you enter therapy with nebulous or undefined goals, you can continue in therapy indefinitely without any real, measurable progress. Life will always give you subjects to talk about and problems to solve. No one is problem-free or has an easy life. How will you know when you are ready to leave therapy if you don't know what you want to accomplish there?

Also be aware that as your therapy progresses, your goals may change. What seemed the focus when you started may change as you have a better understanding of the sources of your discomfort and the resources you have to resolve your problems. You could start out wanting to be more satisfied with your life because you feel you should be. Later, you may decide to make some dramatic changes when you discover your talents, abilities, and strengths. These changes might need support and coaching from your therapist or someone else.

19. Your contract for therapy

In setting your goals for therapy, you are making a contract with your therapist. You are saying what you have come for, what you'd like to accomplish, and what will be the focus of your therapy hours. By doing this at the start, you are making an agreement with your therapist about the terms and limits of the therapy process. Part of this agreement is how long the sessions will be—usually forty-five minutes to an hour, depending on the style of therapy. Some sessions are ninety minutes or more. You should also come to an agreement about fees and a payment schedule. (See topics below.) This contract includes how missed and cancelled sessions will be handled and might include how long you are agreeing to be in therapy, although this may change as your goals change. Once you have selected a therapist, it's a good idea to have a time frame of several weeks or a few months. At the end of this, you can assess your progress and determine whether you want to set new goals or stop the therapy. Keep in mind that you want to establish these ground rules at the beginning of your therapy to avoid some therapy pitfalls.

This agreement, whether verbal or written, can be re-negotiated at any time. A therapist who doesn't want to have such an agreement may be more interested in his/her own advancement than yours. Your request for specific goals indicates that you are taking an active role in your therapy and making choices consciously—a first step into true mental health.

20. Choosing a therapist

Your choice of a therapist should be made with care. Referrals are one of the best sources of therapists. Perhaps you have a friend who was in therapy with someone and you have seen the positive changes he has made because of his therapy. If you have a physician you trust, you might ask her to recommend a psychotherapist, psychologist, or psychiatrist, depending on the nature of your problem. We'll discuss the differences in training below.

You can also call the Mental Health Association in your area and ask for a referral. The counseling services listed in the telephone book will have many therapists to pick from, but this has its risks since you don't know what you are getting or how good the therapists are. In any case, be prepared with a list of questions to ask before embarking on a course of therapy with anyone. It is amazing to me that many people will ask a prospective house painter more questions about their business than they would a doctor or therapist.

Keep in mind that this is an exploration. You are shopping for a therapist. You can change your mind after meeting someone or rule someone out based on a telephone call. If the therapist refuses to take a few minutes to talk to you on the phone or if the only person you can talk to is the receptionist who is pressing you to make an appointment, hang up and call someone else. You are the consumer and you should be able to ask questions.

21. Licensure, credentials, training, experience in specialty or problem.

The therapist you see should have specific training in psychology. In most states, to call yourself a psychologist, psychotherapist, or social worker, you must have a minimum education in psychology and a state license. A psychologist usually has a doctoral degree (Ph.D. or Psy.D.), which is two to four years (or more) past the master's degree. A psychotherapist or social worker has a minimum of a master's degree (M.A. or M.S. or M.S.W.). Psychiatrists are medically trained doctors. They go to medical school to become physicians and then do a residency in psychiatry as their specialty, similar to the way other doctors might take a residency in dermatology or surgery. Psychiatrists are medical doctors first, psychotherapists second. They can prescribe medication and authorize hospitalization while other therapists cannot. The severity of your problem might help you decide whether you want to see a psychiatrist or a psychotherapist whose training has focused more on therapy and the variety of techniques of psychotherapy for talking about problems.

Physicians, in the medical model, will more frequently be thinking in terms of disease and cure. They sometimes have less training in psychotherapy than their counterparts who didn't go to medical school.

A psychoanalyst is someone who has had training at a psychoanalytic institute in the specific procedures of psychoanalysis. She might be a medical doctor (psychiatrist) or a Ph.D. in psychology before beginning psychoanalytic training. This is a rigorous program of several years and includes a personal analysis. Successful completion of that analysis is necessary for one to complete the study.

22. The therapist's own therapy experience

Many people assume that all psychotherapists have had their own therapy or analysis as part of their training. With the exception of psychoanalysts, many people who work in the mental health field have had little or no personal therapy at all. Because they have not examined their own problems and motivations, these can easily spill over into the therapy encounter. A therapist who is unaware of his own motives may project them onto his clients, seeing his own problems in the client where they do not exist. Or a therapist may make interpretations without awareness of how her own desires and wishes impact on her thinking. This is probably one of the biggest flaws in the therapy encounter. This can also happen to therapists who have done personal work in the past but who have lost touch with their own inner drives and desires because they have not continued to examine themselves.

You can ask a prospective therapist what personal therapy they have had and for what length of time. Some therapists will continue in therapy sporadically to supplement their personal supervision as a therapist. This is to their credit. Don't think of the therapist as not being "finished." There is no true finish with personal work though there may be an end of formal therapy. Ideally, we work on ourselves all our lives. There is always room to improve and grow and be more self-aware.

23. Referrals, word of mouth, professional acquaintance.

If you are referred to a therapist by someone else, ask yourself how much you trust this person's judgment, particularly in the area of mental health and personal growth. You might ask why this person is recommending a particular therapist. What are her strong points? Why does this person think the therapist is competent and effective?

There are many psychiatrists who are well known or have established a name for themselves who are still poor therapists. They may be good speakers and entertaining guests on talk shows, but they may lack the ability to work effectively to help you solve a practical problem. Theoretical knowledge is very different from capable actions and interventions in therapy.

If you have a friend who is a therapist, you might want to consult with him or her as a first step to getting professional help. But it is unwise to attempt to maintain both a friendship and a formal therapy relationship with the same person. In some

states, "dual relationships" are a violation of the ethical principles of doing counseling or therapy. A friend can be the best help
in a time of need, but the discussions you have with a friend and
the feelings brought up will not be addressed in friendship, as
they will be in therapy. In some ways, these conversations may be
better because this person is personally committed to you as a
caring friend and does not have a monetary interest in doing
therapy. She knows you and might be able to give you some honest feedback because she has seen you with your problems in
operation. She knows your strengths and your weaknesses and
can help you see yourself more clearly.

On the other hand, she will have feelings for you that may
interfere with her being helpful or as objective as you would like
a therapist to be. Of course, no one is completely objective, not
even therapists. But friendship can further muddy the therapeutic waters.

24. Young therapists and/or those new to the field

People often want their professionals to be experienced. Of
course, anyone with experience started without any experience at
one time. They learned by doing, by making blunders and being
committed to continued learning. Often, new therapists have
humility and an openness because they know they are new and
inexperienced. A therapist working in the field a long time may
be jaded, cynical, or burned out. Some reduce their therapeutic
choices to a few techniques, convinced they are the best ones.
They have seen so many cases that this one seems familiar and
they think they know what's best. They have a few formulas that
they use repeatedly.

Certainly, not all experienced therapists become cynical or do their work by rote, but some do. A new therapist might bring to your therapy fresh ideas, enthusiasm, and hope. Age and experience doesn't always mean quality work.

25. Interviewing a therapist on the phone; questions to ask

Questions to ask a prospective therapist on the telephone should include, but not be limited to:

1. What is your training?
2. Where did you go to school and what year did you graduate?
3. What license(s) do you hold?
4. Do you do short-term or long-term therapy?
5. How do you describe the therapy you do?
6. Briefly, what psychological methods do you use?
7. Do you have a personal philosophy that influences your work? What is it?
8. How much does this cost?
9. Will there be any other costs in the future?—such as lab tests, groups, or special programs I have to buy.
10. How long is a therapy session?
11. How are missed sessions handled? Charged for or not— and under what circumstances?
12. Can you be reached in emergencies and on weekends? How?
13. (If a psychiatrist) Do you prescribe medication?
14. (If not a psychiatrist) Do you recommend medication through a psychiatrist?

15. Are you affiliated with a psychiatrist?
16. Do you take insurance?
17. If I pay directly, can a payment schedule be arranged?
18. How long have you been seeing private clients?—if the therapist is in private practice
19. How long have you worked at this facility?—if the therapist works for an agency. Some agencies have a high turnover of therapists and yours may not be there any longer when you call again for another appointment in two months.
20. Do you set treatment goals? How are these decided?
21. How do you keep up with current trends, research, and developments in the field?
22. Will you see family members with me in the future if I desire it?
23. Have you been in therapy yourself?
24. Have you published and books or papers? Where can I find them?

None of these questions require long explanations or much of the therapist's time. A therapist who is unwilling to answer these questions or wants to analyze why you're asking them is already setting up a dynamic where you, as the client and consumer, are in a one-down position. You are going to pay this person for her services. You should be able to ask questions just as you would any other professional person you would hire—an accountant, attorney, plumber, or painter. Think of the kind of caution you would exercise before you let a carpenter come into your home to work. Would you let someone tear off your roof if you weren't sure he was a reputable businessman?

Remember you're about to let this therapist inside your mind and your feelings. Some therapeutic techniques are very powerful and life changing. You have reason to demonstrate caution and make thoughtful judgments in your choice of a therapist. It's a sign of mental health to do so.

26. Client rights and informed consent

As a patient or client in psychotherapy, you have certain rights that are part of the ethical and moral obligations of this exchange. While some of these are contained in the law in certain states, others are simply listed as guidelines in the codes of ethics of various professional organizations.

These include:

a. The right to privacy—the assurance that what is discussed in therapy will be confidential and that none of the content of your therapy will be revealed to others without your written consent.

b. The right to equal treatment—that you will be given psychotherapy services without regard to your race, religion, class, ethnic group, age, gender, sexual preference, physical condition, attractiveness, or presenting problems.

c. The right to expect that your welfare will be a priority for your therapist—part of the Hippocratic oath of "not for their hurt or for any wrong."

d. The right to be taken seriously and with respect by your therapist, that your concerns or problems will not be treated as trivial, whimsical, or self-indulgent.

e. The right to informed consent. This means that you have a right to be told what procedures the therapist uses and whether these have been explored by other professionals, including knowing what risks and benefits come with the se techniques. This includes your having the freedom to make a choice about participating in certain programs. You have the right to be told what alternate procedures might be used to resolve the issues you bring to therapy.

f.   The right to ask questions at any time during your therapy about your progress and the techniques being used and to get clear answers. This includes asking about the therapist's training or experience in therapeutic methods used.

On the other hand, a therapist will often not answer questions about his/her personal life since these questions lead to conversations about the therapist instead of about you. The therapist might ask instead, "Why do you ask?" exploring your curiosity in terms of your own beliefs and assumptions. The therapist is correct in keeping most of his life separate since he should not be seen as a model for how you should live your life or what your values should be.

Clients often look up to their therapists as they do to a parent and want to model themselves after the therapist. The less you know about the personal details of your therapist's life and life's choices, the more likely you will be to find your own way and make personal choices that are correct for you.

g.   The right to review your records or files at any time.

h.   You have the right to discontinue therapy at any time without any financial obligation for services not received and without any moral or legal liability.

i.   You have a right to know that, by law, your therapist must reveal with or without your permission your intention to do bodily harm to another including if you are abusing a child or an elderly person. Your therapist can also concur with your family members to hospitalize you if you threaten suicide or plan to cause grave bodily harm to yourself or others. (See topic on hospitalization below.) Your therapist may also be required by law to reveal the specific information from your therapy sessions if s/he is ordered by the court to do so.

j.   The right to know what medication your psychotherapist is prescribing (if any and only if s/he is a medical doctor) and the side effects and potential dangers of such medication. You have the right to refuse medication or to consult with your therapist/physician to determine a dosage that has the minimum negative side effects for you.

k.   The right to know that therapy may bring up unpleasant memories, uncomfortable feelings, thoughts, and urges. You have a right to know that these may seem intense or unusual to you and that they are part of the course of therapy and are normal reactions to the material that can surface in discussing your problems, concerns, or hopes for the future.

l.   The right to discuss your goals for therapy and to participate in the design of a treatment plan.

m.   The right to set boundaries and limits on what you will do when asked by the therapist to perform homework or directives, and the right to expect that the therapist will not exploit your vulnerability or neediness in any way.

Some of these will be discussed further below.

Your responsibilities as a patient/client

These include an agreement to attend your scheduled sessions on time. You agree to pay for or make up missed and cancelled sessions according to the agreement you make with your therapist. You agree to make payment in the amount negotiated and in the manner discussed with your therapist such as paying per session, weekly, monthly or through a third party such as an insurance company. Most important, your responsibility is to be as open and honest with your therapist as you can be so that you will get the most out of your investment in time and money.

27. Confidentiality and privacy

When people express their concerns and fears about entering psychotherapy, the issue of confidentiality is often one of the first to surface. They fear that the therapist will talk to others about what they reveal in their therapy sessions. Part of this is the fear that their worries and thoughts and feelings will be considered foolish by the therapist and his professional associates. They might fear that their secrets will be discussed or disclosed to another family member or someone the client knows.

Your therapist is bound by the ethics of the mental health profession to keep your personal information private. In some states, it is against the law to pass any information on to others without written permission of the client. Your therapist will not talk about you or gossip about you without risk to his or her professional license.

Do therapists gossip about clients and neglect their ethical commitments? Some do. Any profession has scoundrels, incompetents, and unethical practitioners. This is another reason why you should choose your therapist wisely. If you go to a therapist who talks about other clients and names them, or reveals what should be confidential information about other clients you know, then you have reason to be concerned. It is wise in such a circumstance to confront the therapist as well as to terminate therapy. This is also true if the therapist's staff makes a comment that reveals knowledge of you from your counseling sessions.

For you to do the work of psychotherapy and get the most benefit from it, you have to feel safe and confident that your disclosures and your records will be treated as confidential information.

28. Respectful, concerned interest in you as a person

Another concern is the understandable desire to be treated with respect. As clients, we don't want to be thought of as customers or as one of hoards of people who come through every day. We don't want to be thought of as only cases or specimens.

Disrespect for your views may be evident in the therapist's tone or the kind of questions s/he raises. "You didn't do that, did you?" Most of us recognize an accusatory or judgmental question when we hear it. We have a physical reaction to the probe, such as a tightness in the chest or gut, a feeling that tells us we have to defend ourselves.

Such questions imply that the therapist knows better than you what is the correct course of action. He feels he knows what you should do or should have done, rather than exploring your reasoning and emotional reactions to your particular situation. Should you have the feeling that the therapist's views or questions are less than respectful of your point of view, speak up and say so. Your therapist's reaction will tell you how much respect he holds for you.

Similarly, as we discussed under client rights, your concerns should be taken seriously and with respect. Your fears or limited skills in certain social situations or work challenges may seem small or unimportant to your therapist, but they are important to you if have come to therapy and paid your money to bring them up.

A good therapist will make every effort to see your concerns as you do, to grasp your problem as you experience it. A good therapist will hear you out instead of jumping in with solutions and suggestions. You, the client, should be the one to set the agenda for what is of concern to you and you should be the one to find your own solutions. The therapist's task is to listen respectfully and give you the opportunity and tools to find new behaviors and new ways to experience your world that will improve your life.

29. Money, fees, and sliding scales

Fees for psychotherapy differ widely depending upon the therapist's training, the area of the country you are in, and the kind of therapy offered. A well-known psychiatrist who has a current and popular book might charge five or more times what a master's level psychotherapist would charge for a similar service. Supply and demand function in the medical profession in much the same way they do in other areas of business. Sometimes, a therapist will reduce their fees at a time when a client is in financial distress due to crises such as job loss or divorce. Other therapists work on a sliding scale, charging a range of fees depending on the client's income and ability to pay. Beginning therapists may charge less than experienced and established therapists with active practices. You can negotiate a fee with most therapists and there is no reason not to if you have a need to do so. However, bargaining for its own sake has no place in a professional encounter.

The fee your therapist charges should be clear from your telephone conversation. If the therapist declines to name a fee, then the first session may be considered a consultation and not be charged for. It would not be fair for you to have a session and then discover after the fact that the fee is more than you can afford to pay. Remember the rules you apply to working with anyone else—you agree to a fee before you contract for service.

In addition, a therapist should not ask you to pay in cash. Such a practice indicates the possibility that s/he is trying to avoid paying income tax on this money. By paying with a check, you have the advantage of a record of payments that can be used to support your filing for insurance and may qualify as a medical tax deduction when you file your own income tax. Be wary of therapists who want to do business "under the table." You might want to question their ethics in other areas as well.

30. Insurance and managed care

Many therapists take insurance or are affiliated with insurance programs. Your health insurance may cover a certain number of sessions for psychotherapy with a dollar limit per year or a lifetime amount for these services. Once you use up your quota of service, you will have to pay for any future therapy on your own. If you have a limit of six or twelve sessions, then this should influence how you choose a therapist. For managed care patients, a therapist who has skills and training in short-term, solution-focused psychotherapy may be a better choice than someone who usually does long-term analytic therapy where clients have many more sessions than the number your insurance allows. On the other hand, you might want to consider paying for you own therapy sessions as you need them.

Also, with a therapist who does not take insurance, you may want to consider paying on your own. Your decision can be based on how much you have and how much you want to invest in improving yourself, just as you do when you pay for any other education or expert counsel.

31. Who pays for your therapy?

Paying for your own therapy is an opportunity to step into being an autonomous and independent adult. When someone else pays for your therapy, you are robbed of the opportunity to value yourself by spending your own money on your own growth. Frequently, a parent or other person who is concerned about someone will offer to pay for therapy. This is a generous offer but can have pitfalls. The person who pays the therapist automatically has an alliance with the therapist. Who sets the agenda? The client in therapy or the person who pays the thera-pist? Clearly, the person in therapy is the one who should make the decisions about what goes on in therapy and what his or her needs are, but money has power. The therapist's acceptance of payment from someone else can be the source of a conflict of interest. As much as possible, it is best that you, the client, pay for your own therapy. When you value yourself enough to spend

money on the kind of personal education that therapy can provide, especially when it means making some other economic sac-
rifices, you will take your therapy more seriously and get more
benefit out of it.

32. Your first session

Some people enter therapy with an enthusiasm to get down to
work and begin the deep processes of uncovering problems, facing past traumas, and revealing character defects. While this may
be admirable, the first session is really a time for assessment for
both the client and the therapist.

As the client, your first session is the time to get your questions answered if they have not been satisfactorily answered on
the telephone. It's a time to see how you feel communicating
with someone who may be a confidant for some period of time.
Does the therapist listen attentively and respectively? Does she
let you finish what you have to say before speaking? Does he take
phone calls during your session? If he does, does he take them
within your hearing range and how does he talk to others? What
is the atmosphere in the office and how are staff and employees
treated? Is this someone you want to open up to? Does she seem
warm and interested or cold an indifferent? Do you find him
patient and supportive or abrupt? How does this initial exchange
feel? Do you feel acceptance and understanding or disapproval
and judgment?

Your first session is an opportunity to see how you experience
a potential therapist and to see if you can work together. If you
have come in with one concern on your mind and the therapist
immediately determines that he knows the original cause and

cure for your problem, you would probably be better off moving on. Instant assessments, based on single causes applied to everyone, cannot be helpful since your problem, while having universal aspects, is individual and unique. Your therapy should be tailored to suit your needs. It should match the way you learn and work with someone else, using your style of understanding and be in the language you find most comfortable.

Not all therapists and clients can work together. Your first session may be your last with this therapist. You may have to shop around to find someone with whom you can establish rapport and comfort in that first session. Your decision to discontinue is not a failure for you or the therapist. Again, when you contract for professional service, it's very important for you to trust and like the person you're working with. In therapy, confidence and comfort are essential for the success of your work together.

Studies have repeatedly demonstrated that it is *the therapeutic relationship more than any school of psychological thought or technique that results in the most improvement.*

33. Ethical standards and professionalism

Mental health organizations and licensing boards have standards of ethical and professional behavior for practitioners. These are spelled out in codes of ethics that the therapist is bound by in order to retain his license and authorization to practice. Such standardized codes provide protection for the client who will have recourse through the courts and/or licensing agencies if these standards are violated. This is one reason why a client incurs additional risks when seeing someone who is not licensed. If a "healer" suggests a course of action or beliefs that turn out to be harmful, where do you turn to get assistance to solve the problem?

Ethical standards prohibit sexual contact between therapist and client under any circumstances. The power differential between client and therapist puts the client in a vulnerable position that can be harmful in the context of sexual intimacy. This prohibition includes having a therapist observe you alone or you and a partner engage in sexual behavior. In addition, a therapist's use of the power of the relationship to exploit or use the client in any way is unethical. The therapist's asking for favors, assistance, or special treatment in the client's field of expertise is a breach of the professional boundary. We will look further at some of these ethical violations in detail in many of the topics in this book. However, if an exchange with your therapist feels like a violation of your boundaries at any time, SAY SO. If you are unsure what the ethical standards are in your situation, ask someone else whom you trust. You might also call your local Mental Health Association and ask to speak to someone who can answer a question about ethics in counseling and therapy.

34. Therapist availability when you are in crisis

There are times in the course of therapy when crises occur. You may have an accident or a death in the family or a sudden worsening of your problem. Your therapist should be available to you at those times or be able to get back to you in a reasonable time frame if you should need her. What is reasonable? That will depend upon the crisis and the arrangement you have with your therapist for handling crises and emergencies. Hopefully, you have already inquired about this in your initial interview of the therapist on the telephone or in person.

If you are the kind of person who needs a lot of support and contact, who needs to talk about your problems and how you are thinking about them from day to day, you might consider what other supports you have in your life. You have a professional relationship with your therapist who has her own life. Some clients want to be able to call whenever they have an insight or a moment of strong feelings. These are events you must learn to endure on your own. You might want to use a journal to continue your personal work between sessions or to prevent yourself from forgetting insights. If something is important, you can talk about it at your next session. Demanding telephone time at every whim is unreasonable and a competent therapist will set limits and boundaries.

Everyone needs others to feel connected. However, your therapist shouldn't be your only source of emotional support and comfort. Part of being a fully functioning human being includes developing and maintaining a variety of relationships that are mutually satisfying.

If your therapist is unavailable when you are in a serious or life-threatening crisis, you should have an alternate plan. Be prepared with someone else you can call or know how to get to an emergency room or crisis center.

35. Scheduling sessions

Therapists in private practice usually have set hours when they see clients. Some will offer evening, early morning, or Saturday hours for the convenience of people who work, but some do not. Part of being mentally healthy for many people includes having some kind of daily agenda, including a work schedule and meeting other obligations. If you work a full-time job and have responsibilities to your family, you may need to find a therapist who has more flexible hours than someone who only works nine to five on weekdays. Alternatively, you might also be able to request some flexibility in your hours at work or your lunch breaks to make time for your therapy hour. Most employers are willing to make these concessions when they are able.

It is important that you take your therapy seriously and make time for it. Your therapy can be a vehicle for you to be more effective in your life. What may seem like a mundane act of simple scheduling of your sessions may reveal your commitment to therapy. It may also expose how you are using therapy to disrupt other areas in your life to indirectly express your discontent— such as missing important meetings at work or being unavailable to family members at important times of the day. You might want to contemplate these issues when scheduling your sessions.

36. Malleable Minds

Human beings show an enormous capacity to change and adapt to even the most horrendous conditions. We live in a wide variety of climates and cultures, of safety and threat, and manage to continue to survive and reproduce our species. Under certain conditions, we are able to change our belief systems, our values, and our loyalties. Things we say we would never do are things we do without hesitation when circumstances change.

With the right combination of persuasion and pressure from inside our minds and from others around us, we can make radical shifts in belief and behavior. Liberals can become conservatives; fundamentalists can become atheists; people who consider themselves honest may some day embezzle money from their companies. Engineers can become artists. Some parents turn into child-killers.

People change. Sometimes they get better and sometimes they get worse. That's a value judgment; what I think might be better you might think is worse. But there is no doubt that people can change dramatically in certain conditions and with certain techniques. Therapy is only one condition that brings about change.

Psychotherapy, especially those specifically using trance-inducing methods like hypnosis, provides a context where we are very open to suggestion. The more willing we are to change and alter our perspective, the more we can improve and gain better contact with our heart's desires.

But, as stated earlier, this same willingness also makes us easy prey to those who might exploit our vulnerabilities or to those who want to indoctrinate us in their beliefs for their personal gain. This malleability or flexibility can be used for our benefit or for our detriment. In later topics, we will further examine the possible risks and benefits that arise from this malleability.

37. Transference and Counter-transference

The transference in therapy refers to the common experience of the client's placing past feelings and experiences he has had with others onto the therapy encounter. Usually these feelings are the ones she has felt most intensely about significant people such as parents, other family members, spouses, lovers. The therapist takes the place of these persons and the old emotions and reactions are now experienced toward the therapist.

As an example, a client may have difficulties with authority figures starting with his parents. He comes to therapy and says he has conflicts with others in his adult life such as employers and teachers. He is then likely to view the therapist as an authority figure. He transfers all these previous feelings of anger, resentment, and rebellious impulses onto the therapist whether the therapist's behavior provokes the client or not. Similarly, any feelings of distrust, dependency, idolization of others will be repeated in the therapy situation. Many different psychological approaches use this opportunity as an important part of the therapy to help the client investigate his pattern of interaction with others. The relationship with the therapist is viewed as another example of the repeating patterns and the psychotherapy setting becomes a re-enactment of the client's major life events.

However, this time, the client has a chance to reflect on the pattern. He can step back and observe what has become a pattern of behavior. He can then choose to make changes in his beliefs and automatic reactions. The client can understand his contribution to the problems in his life when the therapist is not participating in the pattern nor participating in the power struggle that the client perceives.

By monitoring the transference, the client learns about his own reactivity—perhaps how he tends to attribute malice to the therapist's choices or comments. This unthinking response is based on the client's history and is superimposed on current events and may bear no similarity to the original events. The therapist may remind you of your mother, as other women might also remind you of your mother. Therapy teaches you that every person you meet is a unique individual who is different from either of your parents. You can begin to see how you perceive all women or all men the same. You may begin to comprehend how you create situations that replay the interactions of your family of origin.

On the other hand, the therapist is also prone to the same transference feelings. When the therapist projects her feelings onto the client's concerns and problems, it is called *countertransference*. This is exactly the reason why it is important for therapists to have spent time in their own therapy. Having a strong reaction to a client's problems or actions indicates that the therapist has her own demands or desires for the outcome of therapy and the course of action the client should take.

Telltale signs of an unexamined counter-transference is a therapist who yells at you, scolds you, shows impatience or uses humor in a hurtful way. Therapists who telephone their clients or suggest social interactions are acting from their own needs, which have not been sufficiently resolved in their own therapy. At best, this behavior on the part of the therapist will undermine and disrupt the therapy. At worst, it can seriously hurt the client.

38. Falling in love with your therapist

It is commonly believed that clients will fall in love with their therapist. For many people, the therapy encounter is the first time anyone has ever truly listened to their concerns, paid attention to them, taken them seriously. A good therapist will show care and respect, will make an effort to understand how you experience the events and people in your life and why they cause you distress. He will be interested in your beliefs about yourself and others. He will ask you what your hopes and expectations are. He will ask you questions that will challenge you to think of yourself in new ways.

These experiences provide some of the best moments in psychotherapy. The person of the therapist takes on larger-than-life proportions. When you realize you feel better about yourself in the presence of the therapist, it is natural to begin to have strong affectionate feelings toward her. A good and competent therapist will keep her own feelings out of the therapy hour and have other relationships to meet her needs. She will not share her innermost feelings and thoughts with the client the way the client shares hers. This "blank screen" provides a clean slate for the client to fill in the space with her own fantasies and projections. Those might include the belief and hope that the therapist feels the same way about the client and the client feels about the therapist, even if the therapist has no such feelings. But the client, caught up in the powerful feelings of the transference, feels this is love. An experienced therapist knows better than to feel flattered by this attention and doesn't encourage it. Instead, this is another time to look at the client's patterns in relationships and what makes him feel as if he has fallen in love.

39. Interpretations and projections

Part of what therapists do is make *interpretations*. These are comments or questions that are based on a tentative theory the therapist holds about what is happening in the therapy hour or in the client's life. One example might be the client who comes to therapy with intense grief over the loss of a loved one. The client complains that he can't get over this loss although several years have passed and he has other satisfying relationships. His emotional experience doesn't match what he thinks he should feel. One interpretation the therapist could raise is that the client is really having difficulty facing his own mortality that this loss has brought up. Or perhaps the client has some unfinished business with this lost loved one that needs to be completed. Maybe the client wishes he had the opportunity to say something before this person died. Or perhaps he is angry at the person for dying and leaving him and this calls up other times when he has had feelings of being abandoned and rejected.

These are all possible interpretations. They are only a few of many, many possibilities. Sometimes one of these interpretations will resonate with the client with a tingle of recognition. Any one of these might open an avenue for the client or it might stimulate an outpouring of emotion, which the client has stuffed down until now.

Any individual therapist can come up with only a limited number of possible explanations and theories for the client's anguish. All of these come from the therapist who is responding to the client's words, gestures, movements, facial expressions, tone, and pitch. These are sensory-based impressions. The client's eyes may fill with tears and the therapist may interpret this as sadness. The client, however, may get tearful whenever strong emotions come up, including happy or exciting ones. Or the client may cry when she is angry.

In addition to formulating theories of the client based on what the therapist sees and hears, he also responds to his own associations, memories, and emotions in the face of the client's story and emotional display. These, too, will affect the interpretations the therapist suggests.

The therapist has no way of knowing the "truth" of any interpretation unless he asks the client whether this seems correct or not. If the interpretation is delivered tentatively and questioningly, not as a dogmatic statement of any "reality," then the client can feel more free to disagree or offer some variation that is more closely in line with her own experience. Unfortunately, some clients are quick to accept and believe *any* interpretation as a suitable explanation for their dilemma. Clients look for cues from the therapist to agree, hoping for the therapist's approval and a solution to their problems. Often, clients forget that no matter what the therapist offers, it can only be a projection of the therapist's own impressions, thoughts, and feelings onto the experience of the client. For any therapist to believe that the interpretation is "objective" or strictly theoretical is nothing less than a delusion. Bandler and Grinder (1981) go so far as to refer to such interpretations as hallucinations. They may be helpful, but the therapist should recognize them as tentative guesses and not as truths.

This is a basic principle of all communication and is often overlooked. What you hear is not the same as what you believe it to mean. The event is separate from any meaning you place on it. If you don't return my phone call, I can think you hate me, are avoiding me, have something better to do. Or I can think you are forgetful, irresponsible, and self-absorbed. These are interpretations of the event and they may all be wrong. You may be out of town and haven't listened to your messages yet or your answering machine may be broken.

Another situation for an incorrect interpretation might occur if you frown during our conversation. I can assume your facial expression signifies disapproval, confusion, disagreement, or that you are in the process of thinking over what I said. Your frown might be caused by any number of alternatives, including the possibility that you simply have to go to the bathroom. If I automatically assume only one of these possible explanations as *the truth*, I am guessing at your experience. I'm assuming I can be a mind reader. Unless I check it out with you and accept your answer, I am living in my own fantasy of the conversation we're having. None of those possibilities may be true. Or several of them might be true in some combination that only you can explain to me.

The term *projection* is usually used to describe the client's tendency to believe the therapist is having certain feelings or thoughts when these originate in the client. If I tell my therapist I think he's angry with me, perhaps I'm angry with him and I've projected these feelings onto him because I have difficulty expressing and acknowledging my anger. This is called projecting onto the therapist. But the therapist's interpretations are also projections. Unless his statements are strictly sensory-based, such as, "Your voice just got a bit louder," he is making up a story about what it means and therefore projecting his story onto you. A clear indication that the therapist's statement is a projection is when he insists it's correct in spite of your having second thoughts about it.

40. What is resistance?

In some schools of psychotherapy, the concept of resistance refers to the client's unwillingness to examine certain portions of his thoughts, feelings, behavior, or character. The therapist says the client resists an idea or being confronted with another perspective because the client doesn't want to face something about himself. The therapist might suggest that the interpretation is difficult for the client to accept because it upsets his self-image. If I think I'm a nice person, and you say something that reveals my cruelty or my insensitivity, then I might not want to hear what you say. I might resist your suggestion by disagreeing or by not understanding or even by not hearing you at all.

The concept of resistance, then, is centered on the client. It views the behavior as a short-coming in the client, with the client's lack of comprehension seen by the therapist as a conscious or more-often unconscious unwillingness to accept the therapist's idea or interpretation. The client is blamed, in a sense, or further pathologized. In fact, the client's lack of understanding or acceptance is often believed to be proof of the rightness of the interpretation.

Obviously, if the therapist is off base or just plain wrong, then the client's lack of understanding or acceptance of the interpretation is correct, rather than "resistance." Rather than considering that what the therapist is doing is not working, he may persist, telling the client that this is "hard for him to see" or explaining how this concept violates his self-image.

Some schools of therapy (Bandler and Grinder, 1979, 1981) suggest that there is no such thing as resistance. What the therapist is experiencing in her interaction with the client should signal the therapist that she has not presented the information in a way that is comprehensible to the client. In psychodrama, we might say that the therapist hasn't given the client enough warm-up or sufficiently established rapport. The client may be too emotional to be able to switch to a more cognitive or mental frame to think things through. The client may need time to cool down emotionally first.

Another cause of resistance might be the style of delivery for the interpretation. Perhaps the therapist's interpretation is heavy-handed or accusatory. Or perhaps the therapist sounds or appears strange to the client. The therapist may not be speaking the same language of metaphor and symbol. The examples the therapist uses may not be compatible with the client's experience and frame of reference.

Or the interpretation may be totally off the mark.

This view of resistance (or its nonexistence) says the responsibility for the client's lack of understanding lies with the therapist's inability to communicate effectively. The polarity sounds like a choice of blaming either the client or the therapist. Perhaps a more accurate point of view would be some synthesis of the two. There are certainly times when we don't want to hear something—especially something negative about ourselves or about how other people perceive us. We do this to protect ourselves from hurt or anxiety. Sometimes we need time to evaluate and absorb a comment that feels critical.

We can handle these sticky times by telling ourselves we will be more open to other points of view, knowing we can accept or reject whatever we want. At the same time, the therapist can acknowledge that her theories and insightful interpretations may be incorrect for a particular client. Perhaps her method for

conveying the concept isn't working and she needs to try something else.

As a client in therapy, it's your job to let your therapist know
what's working for you and what isn't. If you are confused,
uncomfortable, or feel misunderstood, *say so.* You don't have to
seek approval by going along with whatever the therapist says
because she's the expert.

41. Disagreeing with your therapist

If you disagree with your therapist, it's important to tell her.
Part of getting healthy (as opposed to only "normal") is being
true to yourself and being able to speak your truth. You can say,
"I see it differently." There is no need to get into a power struggle with anyone over a difference of opinion. In psychotherapy,
it is the client and not the therapist who should be the final
authority on what is the correct or most valid way to approach
his problem.

Similarly, the client has to be the one who makes the decisions
for changes and choices. In his own life, the client must be in
charge of what is important and how to implement the insights
gained from therapy.

If you, as the client, disagree with your therapist, this will be a
good time to discover whether the therapist respects your point
of view and sees you as an autonomous adult. If your therapist
tells you that you are in denial because you don't accept his interpretation, you can remind him that his interpretation may be
wrong. An excellent example is one that happens in some
groups. If someone tells you that you are an alcoholic (or a sex
addict, child abuser, or a racist) and you say you don't think you

are, you might be told you are in denial—and you might be in denial. On the other hand, you may know what you are or are not. And if you are not what you've been labeled, then how can you answer the statement without being accused of being in denial? The stronger you defend against the statement and the more reasons you give why you think it isn't true, the more this defense is interpreted as "evidence" for the truth of the interpretation—no matter how off-base it is.

Remember that in therapy, as in all of life, the most important thing is to be true to yourself. It's fine to disagree. After all, you might be correct and provide another point of view for your therapist. And if he insists you are resisting, you might ask him why he needs to be right.

42. Who holds the power and authority?

Many people forget when they go to a professional that they, and not the professional, are the ones in authority. The expert or professional only has the power and authority that *you give*. It's yours to give and it's yours to take back.

Unfortunately, it is the nature of some professional interactions, especially those that make you a client or patient, that both parties have a silent agreement that the professional is in charge. Much of this is part of our culture: we are taught not to question doctors and to not take an active role in our treatment. This happens in educational settings too, where the student is in a one-down position in the power imbalance.

In psychotherapy, it is most important that you take an active and energetic role. Waiting for the therapist to decide on the best course of action or expecting the therapist to come up with solutions to your problems, robs you of the opportunity to take charge of your life. Such passivity puts you in danger of being manipulated and influenced in ways that may not be in your best interest.

You cannot give full consent to any treatment plan unless you know what it is and what the benefits and risks are. Many therapists take on the role of the authority person in the therapeutic relationship automatically. The therapist is the helper and you, the client, are the one needing help. So s/he is the authority and you are the one who has come to be fixed, improved, taught, informed, or enlightened. This power differential can be used for your betterment—as with any expert or teacher whom you pay for information and guidance. But it can also be used for your exploitation. After all, you pay the therapist for your time together. Experts get paid for their time. However, the therapist's financial incentive can also be an obstacle to your progress. The therapist may use the power of his position to tell you that you are not well enough to tackle certain projects or further growth on your own. He may try to persuade you to be hospitalized, to influence you to make certain choices, or prevail upon you to continue your therapy—with him.

Be aware of this power imbalance and its impact on you throughout your therapy. Remember to ask questions and speak your personal point of view and your personal truth. These are the best avenues toward your own mental wellness.

43. Alliances: divide and conquer

In the natural course of therapy, the client forms an partnership with the therapist. This is sometimes called a working alliance. It's that comfortable feeling when people are moving toward a mutual goal and the communication feels clear and reasonable. Often, both therapist and client feel as if they like each other, as if they are making progress, and doing something meaningful.

However, the alliance between therapist and client should not be the only relationship the client has to disclose personal details of emotion and experience. If your therapist suggests that you should no longer talk to others about your problems or progress in therapy, then she may be using the old tactic of "divide and conquer." This is particularly true when she expresses the point of view that all of your other relationships with friends and family are dysfunctional, "sick," and destructive to you. Ask yourself if this is true and what supports this assessment.

If your therapist has a tendency to read malice into the actions of others and tells you these people are harmful, then you might consider what the therapist's motives are. Clearly, it is possible that your family and friends have hurt you either intentionally or unintentionally, but they are still your family and you may want to find a way to deal with them more effectively rather than cut them off. Part of the point of going to therapy is to learn new ways to think and behave so that you can improve these relationships, not to have an exclusive relationship with your therapist. If your therapist isolates you by discouraging other relationships or suggests you cut yourself off from other people with whom you have contact, then you should be alarmed.

Ask yourself, What do I want? What did I come to therapy for? Perhaps you want to improve your marriage and have a better quality of interaction with your mate. Sharing your concerns and the concepts you learn in therapy will help your ability to express yourself as well as improve your relationship, as it does in all relationships. When the therapy relationship becomes more real than the rest of your life, the therapy has gone astray. Maybe your therapist needs you more than you need him.

44. What are the beliefs and values affecting the therapy encounter?

Whatever beliefs you hold, you will bring them with you to therapy. These include your beliefs about yourself, about other people including those you know as well as strangers, and about the world. If you believe the world is an unsafe place and people cannot be trusted, that opens a different focus for the work of therapy than if you believe you cannot trust yourself and you feel incompetent and inadequate.

The beliefs your therapist holds about what it means to be mentally and emotionally healthy will also direct the course of your therapy. If your therapist believes that having an exclusive and sexual relationship with someone of the opposite sex is the true measure of a successful therapy, that will influence the ultimate outcome of your work together. If he emphasizes material success, education, or spiritual growth, these will all determine the turns and direction of your therapy. Your therapist's values are always present in the therapy hour, just as your values are. Whose values impact more on the outcome of therapy will, in large part be up to you. If your values include having several intimate relationships at a time rather than one, or perhaps having a relationship with someone of the same sex, then it's important for you to make these values clear. Perhaps being more successful in your work is your priority in your therapy. You might want to re-examine these values and determine if they are realistic and the best ways for you to expend your energy. Or perhaps you want to change your priorities for your life's purpose. In any case, be aware that your therapist's values, whether they are spiritual, sexual, financial, or about physical health and fitness, will determine the focus, direction, and outcome of your therapy.

This is particularly true when therapists have come to believe that most emotional problems have the same cause.

There are therapists who give bizarre explanations for the suffering of people with depression and anxiety. Some say these people have been abducted by a UFO. Other "fringe" therapists say their patient's present distress began in childhood with their parents' activities as satanists or abusers. Such single-vision therapists see their one "cause" in all distress and often create more problems than they solve. We will look at some of these unusual theories and their consequences below. For now, it is important for you to realize that your therapist is human with personal blind spots and beliefs. Again, ask questions and feel free to disagree. If your voicing another point of view is discouraged or interpreted consistently as resistance or denial, consider moving on.

45. What is your lens on the world?

Whatever you believe, you will find evidence to support your beliefs because your attention tends to concentrate on those observations that confirm your view. If I believe someone doesn't like me, then I will notice every slight, every frown, every shrug; I will interpret these as personal criticism or insults that support my belief in their dislike. I might even completely miss noticing the smiles and compliments. Or I might interpret a compliment as having an ulterior motive or hidden agenda.

These distortions happen to all of us. Becoming aware that our interpretations of our environment may or may not have any basis in reality is the beginning of a healthy skepticism. Our lens on the world governs how we react or make decisions every moment of our lives. Being aware that there are other interpretations and other ways of viewing and understanding the same events can be liberating. At first, it may be confusing because we are so accustomed to believing we are RIGHT. But later, the realization of a variety of interpretations opens a wealth of choices. This gets us unstuck from our old and unsatisfactory patterns. I can choose to see myself as a victim of the neglect and malice of others. Or I can assume that no malice was intended, that other people are simply preoccupied or involved in their own lives and not as absorbed in mine as I am.

46. Black and white thinking

Many people are distressed by seeing the world in black and white. I am either wrong or right. You are either a bad person or a good person. I can do A or I can not do A. That is, do nothing at all. I'm caught between a rock and a hard place. I have only two choices and they are both lousy.

This limiting view prevents you from seeing the many other possible solutions a single problem might have. As an example, if I am not getting along with my partner, I could leave and be alone, enjoying the benefits of solitude and independence. Alternatively, I could leave and search for a new partner, or I could get a secondary, additional partner who satisfies the needs my first one doesn't. I might make this last choice secretively and deceitfully. Or I could attempt to openly persuade my partner that such an addition would be of benefit to both of us. In another approach, I might choose to influence and educate my partner to make changes to improve our communication, our love-making, and our appreciation of one another. I can do this by setting an example by my own behavior. Or I can change my attitude about what my partner does that I dislike and see the benefits such a change offers. I can reframe or reinterpret the meaning of the behavior. If my partner's silence brings up my feeling that he is shutting me out, I can also interpret his silence as time and space for me to think my own thoughts. There are many ways to approach a single problem and many choices beyond the one or two I originally considered. *Good therapy increases your choices.* It does not narrow your view to a single, possible explanation and "cure."

47. Who does the talking?

This is your therapy and you are paying, in part, to be heard. You are also providing for yourself an opportunity to hear yourself. (See "Listening to yourself" below.) When your therapist does most or nearly all of the talking, you are probably not getting heard. If you are getting lectures, it's not therapy. You can go to school for lectures or read books for the information. It's cheaper, more efficient, and doesn't have as many of the built-in dangers of persuasion, influence, and subtle control.

On the other hand, if the therapist doesn't talk at all and lets you do all or nearly all of the talking, you might as well save your money and talk to yourself. Or talk to someone else who is interested in what you have to say and responds to you as a real person.

At the beginning of therapy, it is customary for the client to do most of the talking. This makes sense since the therapist is gathering information and trying to understand what troubles the client and what possible therapeutic or educational courses of action to take. Later in the therapy, the therapist will more often interrupt or ask questions or clarify the interaction. She might reflect back to the client what's been said, point out contradictions or changes in mood. She might indicate that the client is saying one thing but reveals emotions or a tone that is opposite from the ones her words convey. The client, in turn, has an opportunity to respond and reflect on what the therapist said.

In these interactions, there is a balance of intervention and technique with the client's exploration and attempts at understanding. There are pauses and silences when the client has time to think about what's been said and formulate a response based on his feelings and thoughts. These silences are often just as important as the verbal insights and teachings your therapist offers.

48. What do you talk about? What are appropriate or necessary topics in therapy? Who decides on the focus of the therapy?

People entering therapy or considering it often ask what they should talk about. They want to know what the proper topics are and what, perhaps, is off-limits.

What you talk about in therapy is up to you. Most likely, you have something troubling you that you *want* to talk about. What you choose, not your therapist's choice, is the proper subject for you. If you are feeling unhappy or distraught about something in your life, then that is what you should bring up with your therapist. Don't assume you have to tell your life story first.

Perhaps you feel some aspect of your life is out of control or you are not accomplishing what you believe you are capable of. Your thoughts, emotions, or behavior may seem to have a life of their own or they don't seem to be under your power. Your feelings rule your decisions and make you feel trapped. You may feel inadequate or helpless. You may feel an uncontrollable sadness. Perhaps an old guilt haunts you.

You start with any of these subjects, in your own way, with your own style of expression. There is no wrong way for you, as a client, to begin a therapy session. The more you are yourself, the more you freely reveal your concerns, the more quickly you will make progress in understanding and changing your behavior the way you'd like to change it.

Sometimes, as you explain why you've come to therapy, you and the therapist will hear some underlying subjects that may be the basis for your distress. A pattern may emerge of similar problems throughout your life. Though the context changes, you might have the same difficulty repeatedly—making the same mistakes or reacting in a repetitive way, without thinking through your choices. Perhaps you have a history of beginning ambitious projects and then abandoning them just as you get close to completion. Your therapist will point out this pattern to you. Together, you will decide on the focus and what priority each subject has in your movement toward mental health and wholeness.

On occasion, you may feel as if you've come to a session to talk about something specific that has happened in your life, especially if it has occurred since your last session. If your therapist aims you in another direction from the one you want to discuss, ask her why she has redirected the subject. This is your time and you should be the one to set the goals for the therapy and each individual session. If she has taken the reins, ask her why and tell her you have something else in mind. There may be a good reason why she has shifted the direction. Her approach may address your goal and the subject you have in mind, but through a route that isn't clear to you. By asking her, you'll find out what you need to know. You'll also be taking a more active role in your therapy.

49. Having a respectful, attentive listener

One of the most helpful aspects of psychotherapy is having someone listen to you with attention and respect. By itself, experiencing someone who listens empathetically and takes you seriously can have a transformative or curative value. Many of us have come from homes where people talk but no one listens. Our opinions and feelings might have been made fun of or dismissed as stupid, foolish, or dangerous.

To have a caring person listen to what you have to say about your unique experience of the world is life affirming. It feels good.

Stephen R. Covey's fifth habit of *The 7 Habits of Highly Effective People* ("Seek first to understand, then to be understood.") tells us how important it is to understand the other's point of view as well as feeling we are understood. Much more than wanting anyone to help us change our situation and alleviate our pain, we want to know that someone has heard and understood us. This one experience alone can be the beginning of a real shift toward taking our lives in our own hands and making positive changes.

A competent and effective psychotherapist listens carefully to what you have to say and asks questions so that she can have as complete an understanding as possible of your experience and how it affects you. She asks questions to clarify what you are saying; she requests details and specific examples. She doesn't offer a quick fix nor does she dismiss your concerns as unfounded. She doesn't interrupt you with reassurance. She allows you to tell your story completely and in your own way before beginning to intervene with possible ways to work on your problem.

In listening, your therapist demonstrates her compassion and empathy as well as respect for you as a separate and worthy person. This listening alone begins the reparative work of therapy, validating your experience and feeling understood and accepted, thereby helping you to accept yourself.

50. Listening to yourself

Part of what happens in therapy is that you learn to listen to yourself. Many times, we talk but we don't hear what we are saying. We complain that others don't listen to us, but we don't hear ourselves, either. Many of us complain about the same things repeatedly, without changing the circumstances causing our problem until someone says, "You've been saying that for ten years! When are you going to *do* something?"

We also don't hear how we sound to others. We don't hear our contradictions and reversals. We miss the way we change the subject, alter our moods, or launch into monologues that are word-for-word what we have said many times before. We don't hear how disconnected our sentences are and how our thoughts jump around. We don't hear our changes in volume, pitch, and pacing. We may not be aware of our incongruence: how our vocal tone and body language do not match the words we say. For example, we might say we're sad and hurt, but we smile when we say it. Or we say everything is fine and we feel happy, but our voice and face says otherwise.

When we speak in therapy, not only does the therapist listen carefully, but we also begin to listen to ourselves. Sometimes, the therapist assists us in hearing what we say by asking us to repeat something. We might be asked to say it several times, rather than just throwing out an important statement that gets lost in a jumble of many other comments.

The therapist might reflect a single remark back to you, imitating your voice, words, gestures, and facial expressions. This is not to mock you or embarrass you, but to give you an opportunity to hear yourself in a way that you might not experience in the outside world. The therapy encounter helps you to step away from yourself and begin to see how others might experience you.

In this way, the therapist acts as a mirror for the client.

51. Setting boundaries

There are times in therapy when subjects come up that you may not want to talk about. Remember that you have the right to choose what you want to share or not share with your therapist. Ideally, you will feel comfortable enough to share anything without censoring your words and topics, but there may be subject matter you feel is off-limits.

When this happens, you can tell your therapist you'd rather not pursue a particular subject. I can think of a few subjects that might fall into this category, especially if you have sensitive information about others or an organization that you are required by law or by your personal morality to keep confidential.

Your therapist is bound by law and professional ethics to keep the content of your disclosures confidential, but in certain circumstances, this might not be sufficient for you. In cases such as these, it's fine to tell your therapist that a subject is off-limits. Briefly, you can explain why without disclosing anything you don't want to disclose. You might say that you could be willing to consider discussing this at a future date, but that you would prefer to shelve this topic for now. A respectful therapist might ask for more of an explanation, but he will respect your decision. The therapist who badgers you to make disclosures you are not ready to make is violating your boundaries. Be prepared to say so.

On the other hand, clients are often reluctant to talk about the very subjects they need to talk about the most. These may be about the client's family and early memories or feelings of failure. The topics avoided are often those that are the most painful and hurtful experiences of his life. A client may find some information embarrassing or humiliating to disclose.

You might have been taught that certain subjects are only discussed within your family. You may believe some subjects are impolite to talk about with others under *any* circumstances. You might hesitate to talk about your sexual difficulties or to describe them in clear detail so that your therapist can know exactly what you're talking about. You may not want to admit your mistakes and defects of character because you want to look good and you want your therapist to like you. After all, you don't want your therapist to think poorly of you. Right? We wouldn't want our therapists to think we're crazy!

Ironically, the "worse" you are willing to appear in the eyes of your therapist, the more quickly you will be able to make the progress you have come to therapy for. That means, as much as possible, to reveal your full range of thoughts and feelings (and the behaviors that follow them) without censoring yourself. Then you and your therapist can look at what you've revealed and what needs to be done about it—if anything. Self-disclosure may be the best way to get a handle on the problem. You will be surprised to find how often the only thing you need to do about your "problem" is to accept yourself as a human being with all the flaws and imperfections that come with being human. Improving from where you are means you must first see where you are.

52. Language and political correctness

One of the ways we try to look good to others is to watch our speech, grammar, and vocabulary. For the therapist, we might alter our natural rhythms and style of speech from our usual pattern. We might refrain from swearing, using figures of speech and gestures we feel are vulgar, or hold in check the speaking style we would likely use with our friends and family. We try to hide our racism, sexism, and other prejudices. Again, we are doing this to make a good impression, to put up a good front.

However, one of the main purposes of your going to therapy is for you to have the chance to take off your mask. By doing so, you and your therapist get to see you as you really are—in your glory as well as your gloom. What you like and don't like about your real self is the stuff of therapeutic work.

Keeping your mask on will only delay your progress and cost you more time and money. The therapy hour should be the one place where you and your therapist permit you to safely let your hidden self show. This means that you don't censor your language or beliefs even when you have the impulse to. You might say, "I hate to say it, but this is how I really feel…"

The important thing is to get the real stuff out on the table.

Your therapist's job is to help you to reveal yourself to yourself. Therapy is more about what you discover about yourself than about what the therapist discovers about you.

Chances are, he's heard many versions of similar problems. Therapy is for your education and advancement, not his. A therapist who limits your topics or your language because it makes him uncomfortable is imposing a limit on your therapy that will impede your progress or making that progress in your own way. A therapist who is uneasy might speak carefully and send you the message to do the same. He might not want to discuss very emotional topics or he may be uncomfortable with emotional displays. He might tell you that you can't swear, shout, or curse in his office. As quickly as you can, resolve this obstacle with your therapist or find another who will not censor you.

Try not to swear at him on the way out.

53. The interrelationship of thoughts, feelings, behaviors.

One of the ways to look at psychotherapy is to see it as an effort to balance or integrate the inter-relationship of thoughts, feelings, behaviors. Individual schools concentrate on making changes in one of these three elements with the belief and expectation that the other two will follow with changes. Repeated change makes for lasting change, just as we form new habits.

We can imagine these three elements as the points of an equilateral triangle (see figure below).

Thoughts (Cognitions)

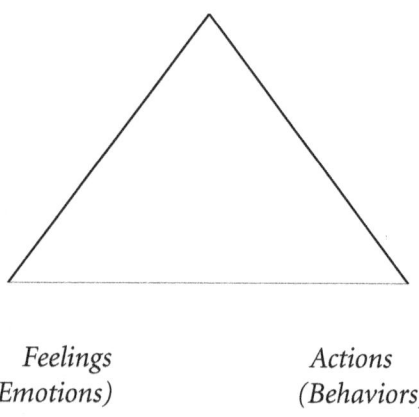

| *Feelings* | *Actions* |
| *(Emotions)* | *(Behaviors)* |

The triangle itself is set in a matrix or background of the client's family and extended family, culture, ethnic group, religious affiliation (or rejection of it), era (time), and cosmology or spirituality. All of these interact with one another so that a change in any one of the three elements will effect the others. Various schools of therapy focus on point of the points of the triangle, with an understanding that they are all related. For example, if I change how I think about something, my behavior and my feelings will both change.

54. Psychological schools: psychoanalytic, psychodynamic, behavioral, cognitive, family systems, existential, spiritual, pastoral, Christian, feminist, eclectic.

There are many different ways to do counseling and conduct psychotherapy—probably as many ways as there are therapists. We will take a quick look at some of the major schools of therapy and then later at some of the particular techniques.

For as long as humans have had words, therapy has been part of what we have done for one another to comfort, educate, and influence each other and to ventilate our feelings. We turn to others when we are emotionally distressed, need guidance, or want to talk through the issues that rattle around our heads and even keep us awake at night. Friends, family, and clergypersons have provided an ear and an opportunity for "therapeutic conversations."

Psychotherapy, as we think of it today, probably began with Sigmund Freud's talking cure of **psychoanalysis**, which is still practiced in various modifications, sometimes called psychoanalytic psychotherapy. In this model, a client will go for therapy several sessions a week, perhaps three to five, usually of forty-five minutes each. The client lies on a couch with the analyst unseen in a chair behind the client's head. The analyst listens to the flow of the client's verbalized thoughts and together they examine the connections, meanings, references, and historical events that have created the client as he is today.

The outcome of this therapy, by studies that have attempted to examine it, has been questionable. The insights gained by the process arrive slowly. The focus is frequently on the client's past and much time is spent on memories, childhood events and traumas, and the client's relationship to his family of origin. Connections are attempted between past and present. The belief is that knowing what past event causes your present behavior is the first step toward change.

The benefit is that the client has an extended period to assimilate the insights gained through this work and to make changes at a deep level, including changes in character, beliefs, and personality. The client comes to know himself well and understands his patterns of relating and coping that began in childhood. The down side is that it is a slow process, often taking many years and a large financial investment. Some people continue in therapy indefinitely and become dependent on the relationship with the therapist rather than using the skills they learned to continue on their own. The technique is also ineffective with some disorders, such as phobias.

Psychodynamic therapy is similar to psychoanalysis in that its focus is on unconscious psychological processes and conflicts, but the therapy may not be as frequent or intense as psychoanalysis. This may be more for practical reasons than because of a difference in philosophy or theory. How it differs in terms of technique or emphasis will depend on the therapist's style. It may also depend on the client's willingness and desire to spend her time discussing past events and possible causes rather than current concerns and goals. A balance between past and present focus is important in any style of therapy.

Behavior therapy usually has the client's problematic behavior as the center of study with less emphasis on what originally produced the behavior or its meaning. If I am afraid of snakes, rather than examine what snakes represent or how my phobia was produced, I could gradually be exposed (systematic desensitization) to harmless snakes and discover I won't be harmed. Or I might observe how snake handlers do their job without the terror that I experience (modeling). Gradually, my terror might diminish. The time a behaviorally-oriented therapist will spend on discussing the whys and wherefores of the phobia or any other behavior will depend on the therapist and the client inter-action, but the usual amount of time is minimal compared with psychodynamic approaches. Behaviorists believe that when a person makes changes in her behavior, the emotions and thoughts attached to the behavior will automatically change as well, though how long or how lasting the change will be is highly variable.

Cognitive therapy addresses the client's thinking (cogni-tions), with the theory that distressing behavior and emotions are produced by a person's belief system. By challenging the client's set patterns of thought, changes are made in the client's behavior and emotions. RET and NLP, discussed later, include aspects of cognitive therapy. For example, perhaps you believe you would experience a devastating embarrassment to make a mistake or admit to a failure. This belief might keep you from expressing yourself honestly, afraid of revealing your short-com-ings. Holding this belief might contribute to your feeling depressed or anxious. You might be fearful of others because they might not like you if they knew your imperfections. Challenging the belief helps you discover that everyone makes mistakes. We learn important information from our so-called failures as much or more than we learn from our successes. This altered belief then has an impact on your behavior. By routinely disputing your beliefs, you might find yourself more and more relaxed about the fumbles of everyday life.

This is an example of *reframing* the problem—telling a different story about the events or giving another more positive interpretation of them. Any event can have many different meanings attributed to it, depending upon who is doing the interpreting and the beliefs they bring to it. You might reframe the meaning of an event, as we did above, or reframe the context. In context reframing, we discover a behavior we dislike is desirable and has value depending on the context. "Stubborn refusal" may be viewed as sensible assertiveness when dealing with pushy telephone solicitors. Reframing is only one of many effective and practical cognitive techniques.

Family systems therapy attends to the interrelationships of the members of a family. Since all behavior is purposeful at some level, the aim is to determine these purposes. If a husband and wife are sometimes in conflict, a child may misbehave suddenly or develop a chronic illness. The function of the child's behavior is to unite the parents to help the child. This interrupts their fighting. Possible motives are explored by the therapist who might then suggest the problem with the child will be resolved when the parents solve their communication problems with each other. The family (or the organization) is seen as a system that has found a way to stay in balance, however precarious and uncomfortable that balance may be. The work of the therapy is to find better ways for the family to accomplish its end—to live together more harmoniously.

Persuading all parties in a family system to cooperate in therapy is not always easy. One member of the family may be singled out as *the sick one* and the others don't want to see their part in contributing to the problem. Going to therapy acknowledges that they have a role in both the creation of the problem *and* its resolution. However, by bringing the family together, the members have an opportunity to learn about the family system, their part in it, and how they are perceived by each other. They can learn more effective ways to communicate and to get their needs met. Each family member may learn how they cue (trigger) another to behave a certain way, just as you may have discovered that you act a certain way only with certain people. The interaction brings out particular traits. When one member of the family begins to change, the others change, too, thereby establishing a healthier basis for family balance.

Existential therapy addresses the meaning we apply to the experiences of our lives. It is based on the concept that distress in the form of depression, anxiety, or other uncomfortable states may be indicators of a lack of meaning and purpose in the individual's life. You may feel alienated from yourself, others, the world, and the god that might have once provided your life with meaning. This school of therapy arose from the philosophical position of existentialism put forth by Kierkegaard, Sartre, and others. It emphasizes personal freedom and responsibility over notions that we are determined by our biological makeup or social and cultural environment. Nothing has meaning except the meaning we give it.

Spiritual therapy may be part of psychological approach to inner work. Among the early psychoanalysts, Carl Jung stressed the idea of spiritual crises being a partial cause of personal torment and unhappiness. The client's finding a spiritual path that is compatible with her other beliefs and desires can be the focus of this therapy. It is essential that the therapist does not impose his own spiritual preferences onto the client. Therapists who try to sell you any religious system are violating your autonomy as well as your religious freedom. Transpersonal psychotherapies may be categorized here.

When a clergyperson is trained in the use of psychological principles, her work is usually referred to as **pastoral counseling**. The counselor may or may not emphasize the spiritual aspects of wholeness and health; she might use any technique or support any psychological theory. The term "pastoral counselor" is often not regulated under the laws that apply to other mental health practitioners. This can sometimes mean limited or unaccredited training and little or no screening for the suitability of these practitioners in the field of mental health. You might come to these people as you would come to a friend, seeking empathy and reassurance rather than psychological expertise.

Christian counseling refers to an approach to therapy that comes out of Biblical teaching and Christian theology. It emphasizes the word and will of god as the source of wisdom over the autonomy and individuality of the client. By definition, the client is not encouraged to find his own way or to establish his own ethics and principles to live by. Rather, these are pro-scribed by the teaching. Depending on the practitioner, a client's difficulties and distress may be intensified rather than resolved. This is especially true when the client is struggling with prob-lems of living in non-traditional relationships or when the client is questioning the dogma of his childhood or if the client is not a Christian.

When a therapist has a set of beliefs that he brings to the ther-apy encounter as the One Truth or the correct way, then the client is robbed of his freedom before he has even begun. This is not true of all therapists who say they are Christian counselors, but the identification poses some ethical and procedural problems. If your therapist is a Christian who believes the Bible should be taken literally, then you are likely to have a problem if your goal in therapy is to improve your relationship with your same-sex lover. You may also be unable to discuss certain issues with your therapist if your choices are in conflict with Christian theology in some other way. You are not likely to get help for the problem you thought you had because it will be re-defined into another problem, perhaps one you didn't think you had, such as bending to god's will rather than accepting your sexual desires and preferences.

However, if your beliefs are in harmony with your Christian (or other sectarian) counselor, then these concerns will not apply to you.

Feminist therapy poses similar problems because the therapist has stated an orientation, an outlook, or viewpoint on the world. Certainly, many of women's problems come out of patriarchy and the male-dominated organization of society. The long-standing, culturally accepted treatment of women has contributed to keeping many women from realizing their full potential and getting respect as an individual. But a focus on only the political issue puts the problem *outside* of the woman rather than mobilizing her energy and attention toward her own resources and power. This is especially true now that women have opened the doors to so many opportunities. Open-mindedness about the source of problems is essential in any therapist.

Certainly, the personal can be political, but we must first begin to make changes in the world by looking at ourselves and taking personal responsibility for our futures.

Eclectic therapists emphasize their ability to draw on many different techniques and psychological schools of thought to be

helpful to individual clients. As time passes, new and more effective techniques are developed. Different clients require different
approaches and methods. What works and makes sense for one
client may be unacceptable or seem like nonsense to another. An
eclectic therapist has a wide range of tools, techniques, and theories to draw from when working with a variety of clients. She
uses what works and lets the client be her guide for choosing an
approach or a tone for the work.

55. Couples counseling or relationship therapy

Couples come for therapy when they believe their relationships are in jeopardy. Frequently, they wait too long before getting assistance to break out of a pattern of poor communication,
control, manipulation, and negative interactions. The longer
they wait, the harder it is to restore good feelings between them,
but it is never too late to ask for help. Much of the work of couples counseling is educational, teaching the partners to speak
and listen respectfully to each other, to return to kindness, and to
remember what drew them to each other. Couples in conflict
have often forgotten what brought them together and why they
fell in love. Therapy, in part, attempts to restore those good feelings and desires for each other.

Therapists who do couples counseling are sometimes licensed
as marriage and family therapists (LMFT). An individual therapist working alone may do couples counseling or might work
with another therapist. This sometimes reduces the tendency of
one partner in the couple to feel that the therapist is aligned with
the other partner. But those concerns can be dealt with in couples counseling since issues of jealousy, rivalry, and loyalty are

some of the most important subjects to deal with when working with couples.

56. Gay, bisexual, and polyamorous therapists

You may believe the sexual orientation of your therapist is important for proper treatment of your problem. This is occasionally true, especially when you are living outside traditional, mainstream lifestyles. You might consider choosing a therapist who, like you, is gay, bisexual, or polyamorous. Whatever your therapist's sexual preference and orientation, he or she should at least be friendly to these lifestyles if you want to talk about them.

Polyamory is sometimes considered a sexual orientation. Polyamorous people are those who want to have sexual and love relationships with more than one person. They may be gay, straight, or bisexual and these relationships may be simultaneous or not. Polyamory is about being open and honest in relationships, not about cheating on your partner or being deceitful about your other sexual partners. This is also called responsible non-monogamy. When three or more people agree to have a relationship with only those in their group, this is sometimes referred to as polyfidelity.

If you believe one of these lifestyles is correct for you and your therapist sees it as dysfunctional or pathological behavior, then that's a big clue to find a therapist who is open to alternative lifestyles. This conflict may also come up if you don't share the therapist's views about living styles such as communal or cooperative living.

57. Directive vs. non-directive therapies

Some therapists refer to themselves as being non-directive. Other therapists say they are objective and can see things unclouded by the client's confusions. In fact, therapists simply have different clouds. There is no such thing as objectivity. In any observation and evaluation, we bring our past, our personalities, our experience, and our unique way of comprehending the world. Not even a photo is objective. The angle, lighting, and composition will have an effect on how it will be received by the observer. A good photographer knows this.

So in therapy, every uh-huh, every question, and every head nod is directive, encouraging the client to follow one avenue of exploration rather than another. No matter how little the therapist says or intervenes, she will be influencing the path and the outcome of your therapy. Good therapists are fully aware of the power of the therapy exchange and are willing to admit their biases and own their own projections and interpretations. There is no way to offer an interpretation such as, "This could mean…." without it being a directive statement. And it is even more directive and powerful coming from a therapist rather than anyone else in the client's life because of the nature of the therapy situation and its power imbalance.

Therapists who are aware that all communication is about influence are willing to offer their comments and questions while being conscious of their power to persuade and direct. Everything that is said can modify, change, and induce the client to behave and think in new ways. This is both a benefit and a risk of psychotherapy. The therapist who denies his influence is dangerous because he may be using his power unwisely and unconsciously. In this way, he may be using it to meet his own needs rather than the client's. While all therapy is directive to some extent, some are potentially more directive than others.

58. Advice and guidance

Some therapists give advice. There are those who say that advice-giving is not psychotherapy, but should be more accurately called counseling or guidance, but the lines are blurry, as any honest psychotherapist will admit.

Therapists often suggest another way for a client to think or feel about a problem. The therapist might make specific suggestions for courses of action, recommending what she thinks would be better for the client. Such advice may be helpful or not. After all, because the therapist can never be truly objective, her advice will come from her own values and preferences. While your inclination may be to forgive and make peace, your therapist's inclination might be to confront and ask for an apology and compensation. Or vice versa.

In general, it is not the therapist's job to give you advice or guidance though that seems to be one of the inevitable outcomes of therapy regardless of the theory and intent. Just as all therapy is directive to some extent, all therapy has some quality of advice-giving. You, as the client, don't have to take anyone's advice, no matter how well meaning and no matter how credible or professional the source. If you feel compelled to follow your therapist's advice because you believe that's what you're paying for, then remind yourself that you are not paying for advice—or at least you shouldn't be. Good therapy is about finding your own way and doing what you know is best for you. The therapist can make suggestions and ask you to experiment with alternative behavior and interpretations of your experiences, but *it is up to you to live your own life*. After all, one of the goals of psychotherapy is to be more personally responsible and autonomous, not dependant on others for guidance or advice or direction.

59. For Your Own Good

The problem of advice-giving is evident when a therapist is insistent that the client take a particular course of action. Such pressure from a therapist is coercive and manipulative. If the therapist tells you to do anything and adds that he is telling you "for your own good," remember how often that phrase has been used to mask what we know is clearly abusive behavior. This is true in therapy as well as in families and other relationships. The only one who knows what's for your own good is you. Telling you that you are in denial or resistant or self-destructive isn't helpful. If any of those assessments are accurate, you'll discover them yourself.

In particular, such pressure from any therapist would make me wonder what the therapist has at stake to push a particular outcome. Why such a heavy-handed style? What does the therapist have to gain if you follow his advice?

You might find it better "for your own good" to see another therapist who demonstrates more compassion, empathy, and respect rather than power, control, and domination.

60. Advice outside of therapist's area of expertise

Clients often see their therapists as wise and helpful. This is part of the positive transference we discussed earlier. Therapists seem to understand and to have access to good choices and decisions that may seem out of reach to a new client. For this reason, the client often seeks out the therapist's advice in areas that are completely outside of the therapist's training and experience. The client wants the therapist to critique his writing, to advise him about an income tax problem, to direct him in his home repairs. In the glow of adoration, the client sometimes reverts to a child-like trust and innocence. He forgets that the therapist has specific training in one field and isn't all-knowing and a source of all wisdom.

Further, the therapist, because of his own needs, might bask in the affection, admiration, and awe the client offers. She might offer advice and direction when she should really be referring the client to a professional in the area the client has questions about. Should you find yourself asking for advice or find your therapist offering suggestions about situations removed from psychology, ask yourself (as a good friend once said to me), "Would you take medical advice from your stock broker?"

Therapists don't know everything about everything, though some of them may pretend to. Get the right professional for the right job.

61. Confrontations and interventions: Is it tough love or abuse?

Some therapists will intervene in the course of therapy in a strong and direct way. They may announce that a certain change or behavior is a requirement for continuing therapy. Such interventions might be, "I cannot continue to see you if you continue to use drugs." Many people would see this as a positive request. Perhaps this kind of firm stand is exactly what the client needs to stop using drugs. The therapist is applying the power of his authority and the attachment and affection of the client to push the client into making a healthy change. The statement conveys caring and emphasizes the importance of the change. The client might feel as though she can't go on without the therapist and this ultimatum forces the client to see that she can only go on without drugs. She might feel that both the therapist and her drugs are "life-lines" when, in fact, the drugs are destroying her and preventing her from having relationships as a conscious adult.

This kind of intervention can backfire if the therapeutic alliance isn't strong or if the client needs other kinds of support to break the habit or to do whatever the therapist has required (rather than suggested). The client might interpret the request as one more example of love that is conditional. She may feel manipulated or controlled, or rebel against the therapist into more destructive and life-threatening behavior.

Any intervention must be used sensibly and with sensitivity to the client's needs and style. Ultimately, it is up to the client to make changes at his own pace and in his own way. Forcing the client "for his own good" can undermine his autonomy and sense of freedom. The client may come to rely on the therapist for making other similar decisions in the future instead of learning to exercise his own will and personal integrity. The therapist may be seen as a good parent at best, or may be perceived, sometimes with good cause, as using this intervention as a way to express hostility toward the client.

In some styles of therapy, very confrontational language and punishment may be used, especially in some in-patient facilities. It is important for people who are considering a specific form of therapy to know what works for them. Do you respond more positively to threats and anger or to encouragement and nurturing? How do you feel when someone calls you names, shouts, or belittles you? Does this make you want to do better or recoil?

Though some people say they have benefited from such a "tough love" approach, I have a personal philosophical objection to some of these methods. They can be humiliating and demeaning. Therapists who use them are poor role models for mature, respectful relationships. They are poor examples for the client who is trying to develop more effective ways to deal with others. The client may want to learn how to be more assertive with consideration for the feelings of others. Emotional and physical violence cannot make a good foundation to build a more loving world where people respect and help each other to grow.

I acknowledge that I'm sharing a personal value here. Yours may be different. You must decide for yourself if your therapist's or your family's interventions are helpful to you or not. As discussed already, it's up to you to participate in setting the tone of therapy and letting your therapist know what your boundaries are.

62. Racism, sexism, and stereotypes

Therapists are human beings just like everyone else. They come to the therapy interview with their own beliefs and expectations, just as we all do. They have a history of experience and indoctrination from their own families, cultures, religious and political affiliations. Many times, this will include stereotypes about other ethnic origins, religions, races, or certain groups of people. They may have standards for what they believe a healthy man or woman should be. As educated and aware persons, therapists like to think of themselves as being above the human flaws of racism and sexism, but these beliefs and expectations come to all of us early. Sometimes, our prejudice is so ingrained and so much a part of our lens on the world that we don't even know it's there, like the fish that doesn't see the water he's in.

As a client, you may be aware of your own prejudices. This may be a concern you would like to address in therapy. You may want to move in a more egalitarian direction to see people as individuals rather than as what you expect them to be because of their membership in a particular group. Should your therapist hold a belief that is the same as the one you want to shed, you may have a hard time making progress. Your therapist might believe that a woman's happiness is dependent upon her being married or that a man must have financial success to demonstrate his mental well being. Any of the therapist's preconceived belief systems about particular issues can impair your work in these areas. Any bias might make it harder for you to transcend the cultural myths and boundaries about what it means to be happy rather than afford you the opportunity to discover fully who you are.

There will be times when you will want to object to what you perceive is your therapist's racism, sexism, nationalism or other bias. Perhaps racism is in *your* perception rather than in your therapist, but it is important for you to open these doors no matter how uncomfortable they make you feel.

This, in part, is the very work of therapy—confronting your beliefs and emotional reactions as well as those of others so that you can communicate clearly and honestly. If you are to do that outside of the therapy room, then you must begin with confronting your own racism and sexism and that which you may see in your therapist.

If it is clear that your therapist is closed to examining these issues rather than looking upon them as "givens," you might consider choosing a therapist who will help you with these concerns more directly. A therapist of the race, group, or gender you are struggling with might provide an excellent opportunity to deal with these issues.

63. Secrets and elitism

There are aspects of therapy that create a secret, special environment for both the therapist and client. As we've seen, the client may be sharing himself openly for the first time. He may be relating experiences, beliefs, and feelings he has never told anyone before. On occasion, the therapist will share herself, too, perhaps relating to what the client is saying in a personal way. These disclosures can improve rapport as well as offer the client a sense that he is not alone in his perceptions.

On the other hand, when a therapist shares secrets that he would not ordinarily tell others, he is creating a situation that can be harmful to the client. If these secrets are not something the therapist would say in front of a public audience or if he asks the client to keep the secret confidential, he is creating a bond that will undermine the client's independence and autonomy. The client may feel special and privileged to have this information, but it will also inhibit the client from talking about his experience in therapy with others. Discussion with others outside of the therapy may be needed, especially when the therapy goes awry and is meeting the needs of the therapist instead of those of the client. By telling the client what he can and cannot talk about with others, the therapist has increased his power over the client. Further, because the client often looks up to a therapist as a role model or idealizes him, the nature of the secret may not be seen in the same way it would be if the person were a peer. Both therapist and client may share the same experiences and guilt, but the way they integrate or resolve these issues may be quite different.

Out of this dynamic of secret-telling, a sense of "we are special" may arise, fostering elitism. This self-inflation of both the therapist and the client is dangerous to personal growth. One of the goals of therapy is to see ourselves as human and equal to other humans, feeling empathy and compassion because they share the same struggles in living. Such elitism can only lead to arrogance and alienation from others.

64. Cosmology and *psychotheology*

Several times, we have touched on how the therapist's beliefs will affect the client and the course of the therapy. Most people don't inquire into a therapist's beliefs when entering therapy. We assume or hope they will be left outside of the therapy room and many of those beliefs may be. On the other hand, some "therapies" center around specific cosmologies. There are those who hold a single, dominant belief and see therapy only through that lens. Some examples follow.

There are therapists (and those working within the therapeutic community under other titles) who maintain that the planet Earth is regularly being visited by alien beings from a variety of locations in the universe, most of them outside our solar system. These aliens are believed to routinely abduct people, including children, to perform mostly sexual experiments on them such as removing eggs and sperm. They then return them to their beds or cars. Those who say they have been abducted have only fragments of images of these events. They believe they have repressed the memories or have had them repressed by these advanced beings.

Therefore, these therapists believe, the common distressing feelings of anxiety, depression, and dissatisfaction are brought on by these abductions. This is especially true, they believe, for people who have been abducted repeatedly since childhood. Additionally, they claim the government is aware of the kidnappings and has covered up as much as possible to prevent a mass uprising of terror and outrage. Among other symptoms, therapists claim that abductees frequently have chronic nasal problems from implants in their noses, placed by aliens to monitor these persons' movements and behavior.

Therapy with therapists who believe these ideas centers on "remembering" this trauma, which is necessary to lift the anxiety and depression, from which so many people suffer. UFOs, they say, are a reality and anyone who dismisses them as foolishness is in denial and probably an abductee himself.

Similarly, another belief system for some therapists states that people who come to therapy with depression and discord in their relationships, or unhappy feelings about their child-hood were most likely abused by their parents. They may not remember the abuse because they had to dissociate from these experiences in order to remain in their childhood household rather than face the fear of being thrown out. According to this school of thought, the less you remember of your childhood, the more likely it is that you were abused, perhaps sexually abused. They will say that the more you hold onto a belief that you had a normal or happy childhood, the more probable that you are in denial of the real traumatic events of your past. Further, if you have some discomfort around sexuality or inti-macy (and who doesn't, at some point in their lives?), this is considered evidence of your having being sexually molested. Likely, you have repressed all memory of the event. Since many children are abused by their parents, it is likely you were too. If you feel as if you were abused or neglected, then you probably were. (Bass, 1988)

The more severe your problems, fears, and anxieties, the more elaborate these stories of "explanation" become. The sexual abuse stories frequently become stories of Satanism, exotic rituals with dark sexuality, incest, murder, animal abuse, and cannibalism.

The practitioners (I hesitate to call them therapists even when they have credentials) of these single-focused treatments will fre-quently use hypnosis and group hypnosis to elicit these stories of abduction and abuse. In a setting where the therapist "knows better" and others are complying by coming up with these sto-

ries, it is likely that you, too, will begin to believe similar encounters have happened to you. You are especially likely to believe if
you are told that this method is the only way for you to get well.
Peer pressure, even for educated, sensible adults can be influen-
tial in more ways than most of us realize.

Schools of psychology sometimes border on the beliefs systems we see in religious movements, also called "true believers."
(Hoffer) Richard Bandler and John Grinder (1981), quoting
Gregory Bateson, call this belief in the truth of a particular
model of psychotherapy a "psychotheology."

Therapists occasionally forget that the theories they use are
only ways to talk about people's experiences (constructs), not
Truths or Reality. If the therapist has been trained in a particular
school, he might believe strongly. His interpretations and explanations will reflect these beliefs.

A Freudian might believe the origin of certain problem behaviors is in the client's sexual drive or result from the experience of
early toilet training. A Jungian might explain the same client's
dilemmas as part of a quest for spiritual wholeness. Other therapists might stress the importance of your ordinal position in the
family, such as being a first born child or the baby of the family.

Other cosmologies or beliefs about how the universe works
are astrology, reincarnation, the existence of evil spirits, the
influence of Satan, the widespread occurrence of certain viruses,
or the hidden evils inside the distressed person. Any of these
may be helpful if they cause you, the client, to think in new
ways, to question your old patterns of behavior and thinking
that are no longer working for you. But if they restrict your freedom of choice or encourage a passivity because "That's the way
I am," then I see these "explanations" as worse than unhelpful.

You may find yourself feeling more stuck and helpless than when you started.

Occasionally, I will hear someone say they talked to a psychic or astrologer and were told that the relationship or professional success they long for will come to them in two years. Waiting for this inevitable outcome, they take less action in their lives to make happen what they want to happen. This can lead to fatalism and determinism, which may prevent the person from taking an active role in her own life. Frequently, this passivity leads to more helplessness and depression instead of greater feelings of personal power and competence.

If your therapist's beliefs seem "way out there," let your critical mind mull over these ideas and apply your own logic and common sense. Ask yourself if these methods are helpful to you or if you feel worse. Then choose your course of action.

65. Religion and spirituality in psychotherapy

In recent years, there has been a return to questions about spirituality and the Big Questions of Life:

Why am I here? What is my purpose or mission?
What do I need to learn?
How shall I live?
How shall I love?
What will I leave on the planet when I am gone?
How will I be remembered?
How do I *want* to be remembered?

Stephen R. Covey sums it up well—we are here "to live, to love, to learn, to leave a legacy."

Religious and spiritual beliefs are more frequently being addressed in psychotherapy. If your distress is partly due to confusion about your spiritual nature or your spiritual quest, then these issues are bound to come up in your therapy sessions. What your therapist believes will make a difference, no matter how "objective" he attempts to be. How you and your therapist make meaning out of life's struggles and joys will depend upon what each of you believes. As we discussed earlier, Christian therapists or those with other sectarian theological beliefs will color and interpret your concerns through their specific lens.

Should you want to do spiritual work in your therapy, be aware that your therapist's answers are not The Answers. If you ask ten therapists the same questions of life's meanings, you will get ten different answers. What the therapist believes is not important. Your work as a client is to find your own way toward a belief system that you find acceptable. Ideally, it will be flexible enough to be shaped by your changing needs as you increase your knowledge and experience through your lifetime.

The problem of mixing religion and psychotherapy comes when religious dogma narrows a person's choices. Some religions say they teach god's will. They circumscribe a narrow set of behaviors as "proper and necessary." They may use guilt and the threat of god's punishment as well as peer pressure to produce conformity among the faithful. Of course, early religious training that was dogmatic is often the cause of psychological distress in later life. It has become a common joke for people to refer to themselves as "recovering Catholics" or "recovering Baptists."

Erich Fromm, in *Psychoanalysis and Religion* (1950) reminds us that religion can also be a vehicle to enhance self-knowledge, self-awareness, and the capacity to love each other when the religion is not dogmatic and punishing. Both psychotherapy and religion can focus on the "care of the soul," however you define it.

66. Hypnosis

Hypnosis refers to the variety of techniques that deliberately create an altered state of consciousness or a trance. You can hypnotize yourself or be hypnotized by someone else. You can also slip into a trance automatically without being aware of it. Most of us have had the experience of "spacing out" while driving, walking, or watching television. You can be in trance when you are lost in thought, reading, or having a waking fantasy. Repetitive motions like running, swimming, knitting, washing dishes, or chopping vegetables are likely to put you into a trance. So might chanting, dancing, marching, praying, and making love.

Because there are so many different altered states, it's impossible to talk about them briefly. What is important to know in the context of therapy is that hypnosis can be used as a therapeutic tool. The client may wish to increase or decrease a specific behavior and certain techniques of hypnosis can facilitate those changes. These changes may be enduring or not, depending on how thoroughly the deeper needs and desires are accessed and satisfied.

For example, if I bite my nails because I'm nervous in certain settings, then perhaps I need to learn other, more effective coping mechanisms to alleviate my anxiety. I can learn ways to challenge the thoughts that crank up my anxiety. I might learn relaxation techniques or I can examine the specific circumstances when I bite my nails—perhaps because I fear I am inadequate to the task at hand. Hypnosis can help to remove some of the blocks to change, but it will likely be longer-lasting if the various components of the problem behavior are also addressed individually, such as skill-training for the circumstances that make me nervous or anxious.

On the other hand, it is important to know that hypnosis creates a state where the person being hypnotized is very suggestible. That is, he is quick to accept suggestions and ideas made by others and then believe these ideas are his own thoughts. This acceptance is even more likely if the person speaking is admired, loved, or seen as an authority. Of course, your willingness to be open can be helpful if what is suggested to you is what you want to accomplish and will improve you in ways *you have chosen.* If, however, the suggestion is to be more devoted or submissive to the person giving the hypnotic suggestion, you might find yourself selling flowers for the guru instead.

Hypnosis can be a powerful and helpful avenue when the client has full participation in the outcome and the kinds of suggestions being made. To believe that your hypnotist is automatically working for you highest good may be naïve and may put you in danger, particularly when practitioners are not licensed as mental health workers. Again, make sure your goals and the interests of your therapist are compatible. If you have a doubt, ask questions, inquire of others, and trust your feelings.

There are those who maintain that there is no such thing as hypnosis. (Baker, 1990) Others say that we are all in trance all the time and that patients arrive at a therapy session already in trance. The work of therapy, then, is to help the person get out of the trance he has put himself in. (Wolinsky, 1991) Some people say our acceptance of our daily lives is a kind of consensus trance. These criticisms may be more of an example of a conflict of terminology than the reality of trance experiences.

Having control over our trances by being aware of them or changing our trances as we wish for our own needs may be another goal of therapy.

Remember that guided imagery and some relaxation procedures can lead to greater suggestibility. We'll address this again when we look at techniques used at large group seminars.

67. Regression, past life therapy, and reincarnation

In recent years, more and more practitioners are using regression therapy as a therapeutic tool. The enormous success of Brian Weiss's *Many Lives, Many Masters* and subsequent books has brought about increased interest in Eastern philosophies, especially an interest in reincarnation. This appeal may be due, in part, with the dissatisfaction many people feel about the religion they grew up with. Out of a desire to fill this spiritual void, other beliefs have appeal. Reincarnation offers the idea that we will have many lives and many chances to improve and correct our defects, to resolve our relationships. Believing in reincarnation can remove some of the sting of our mortality and fears of death.

Under individual or group hypnosis, people are asked to "travel" back to a time when their problems were created. The experience people will have depends upon the beliefs they bring to this experience and the beliefs and suggestions made by the therapist. By now, nearly everyone in the modern world has heard of past life therapy and has seen some version of it on television and film. We have an idea about how to behave and what we might "remember" of a past life or of our early childhoods. This expectation could shape our experience and beliefs about what it means. The therapist's belief in the reality of reincarnation or the value he holds of remembering traumas from past lives might also impact upon the kind of "memories" we will have.

What happens to many people in this circumstance is that they have an experience that they interpret, in the context of the therapy, as a memory. Perhaps they re-experience a childhood beating around the head and ears. Or perhaps they experience a past life when they were present at a huge and deafening explosion. This experience is then used as an explanation of certain fears or chronic physical illness such as problems with hearing.

Did these events really occur? Might they be made up? Might the memories be a combination of truth and fiction, with the person filling in the blanks and trying to make sense of fragments and images? This confabulation of memories is something all of us do.

But if we are to believe that we are the products of our past and our past lives, what is therapeutic in that if we don't move on or *change*? If we are to make changes and improvements for the future, then we must *learn* from our past mistakes and traumas. Instead of seeing ourselves as passive victims of circumstance, I believe the goal should be to have a greater sense of agency and mastery. It must increase our sense of personal power. We begin to see ourselves less as victims or sufferers and more responsible for what happens to us in the future.

That is, the best way to have more choices and feel in charge of my own life is to exercise all the freedom I have in any circumstance. This includes the choice of how I interpret what happens to me and what I can learn from the experience rather than letting it define me. I can interpret it—make meaning of it—in many different ways. And next time, I can do it differently because I claim my power. I can refuse to be a victim.

68. Inner child work

One of the trends in the last twenty years of psychotherapy is inner child work. Since nearly every one of us grows up feeling as though we've had a less than perfect childhood, we come into adulthood with wounds. As adults with resources we didn't have as a child, we can look back on these hurts and understand the limits of our abilities. As children, when we felt ignored or trivialized or otherwise emotionally abused, we didn't have the words or the ability to express our feelings or speak up for our rights. We may have been severely mistreated or neglected. Some of us *were* beaten or sexually abused.

One method for healing these wounds is to contact the wounded child within us to complete and heal ourselves. This is done through guided exercises of writing, movement, drawing, and dialoguing with our inner child. We express some of the emotions that we have never expressed before.

For some people this is helpful and brings closure to events of the past that may have created obstacles in the present. We can comprehend that our habits and behavior patterns served us well as children, but we have more resources and understanding now as adults. We don't have to behave as we did as children; we can change the patterns. We can speak our truth and express our feelings with skill and clarity we didn't have as a child. This work can foster changes to live more effectively and be at peace with our past.

The goal of this work is not to increase our feelings of victimization or to blame our primary caretakers from our childhood. Getting stuck on doing inner child work and staying with the pain is not helpful. Rather, these techniques are vehicles to get complete with the past and to move into a more hopeful future.

69. Repressed/recovered memories and false memory syndrome

The controversy over memory continues. How does memory work? How do I know what I remember is true and accurate?

Generally, it is neither. Many people believe the entire history of our lives is recorded accurately, as if on videotape, and remains in our heads for a lifetime. All we have to do is follow a procedure or undergo the right hypnosis and the memories will be available to us accurately and vividly.

But memory simply doesn't work that way. Our memories are a mixture of images of real events, our emotions that color how we remember them, stories others have told, and changes in perception over time. Each time we tell a story from our history, it changes a little. Try comparing an ordinary (non-traumatic) memory with someone who was present at a specific event. Choose something that didn't have a lot of emotion attached to it and each of you write the story in chronological order. Then compare stories. Even without trauma or terror, the stories will likely be very different, with different details, focus, and meanings attached. The sequence of events might be different or the tone surrounding the event will be perceived differently.

Probably, each of you will be sure of the "rightness" of your memory, although you may have no particular need to be right. There is no accusation or implication of abuse, but you're sure that *your* memory is correct.

As discussed above, one of the "single-minded" therapies commonly used today is to see all of the patient's symptoms as evidence of repressed childhood trauma, especially sexual trauma. Because many children and young people are abused by parents and other trusted figures of authority (teachers, clergy, therapists, scout leaders), it is difficult to sort out the truth. Perpetrators of abuse often don't want to admit their transgressions. This is even more true when the consequences of admission may cost them the loss of their freedom and financial destruction as well as public shame. When offenders already know what they have done, the public admission and apology that the victim seeks may destroy lives.

On the other hand, the victim of the abuse may have spent much of his life wondering if he was crazy, if he imagined what happened. Unless the event is corroborated by other evidence such as other victims, medical records, and witnesses, he, too, may doubt whether it really happened. Where talking to a perpetrator may bring closure, false accusations may also bring ruin to everyone involved.

The controversy is made worse when memories are elicited *only* in the context of therapy by therapists who insist that recovering the memories of trauma is the *only* way to heal or who maintain that the abuse is the only possible cause for the client's symptoms and distress.

Some therapists maintain that the only "truth" that matters is the one the client believes in. This is fine if I interpret some behavior of my parent as harmful and then stay with the work of examining why I see it this way or what other interpretations I might have. I can try to heal this wound by protecting myself from others who might harm me in similar ways. But if a singular belief is encouraged by my therapist, I may never be able to interpret my feelings and impressions in any other way.

Part of the work of quality therapy encourages clients to see there are many ways to tell the story of their history and many ways to interpret motivation. Good therapy introduces the concept of ambiguity and the flexibility of perception. I can always reframe the events. If I feel that I've been abused, then I can, within the context of therapy, explore all the layers of meaning that might have. Other people would see and experience the same event differently. Perhaps my attribution of malice to the intention of my parents is unfounded. My story, as well as the therapist's story of the events, may be wrong.

Insisting on believing "the one truth" that parents harmed us irrevocably can lead me into dangerous territory. If my beliefs about my past lead me to take action through the courts, then the reality, the Truth, of these accusations becomes very important. If I get an attorney and call the authorities and begin a civil or criminal action, it matters very much if my parent *actually* abused me (sexually or otherwise) rather than my using this as a metaphor to express my distress and childhood frustrations.

We are already seeing cases of people who have made such accusations at great emotional and financial cost to everyone involved. Many of these clients recant or retract their stories after they have some time away from their therapists. They come to question the authenticity of their "memories" that came up *only* in therapy. This is notably true for people who never had a memory of sexual abuse before they attended therapy or before they were in group therapy with other victims who told stories of abuse. Such group settings of "victims" or "survivors" sometimes prompt everyone to tell more and more horrific stories. (Ofshe, Singer, Loftus, Yapko)

If your memories surfaced only within the context of therapy, you might have reason to wonder about their function as well as their accuracy. If they surfaced only during hypnosis and guided imagery, you have even more cause to wonder. As we have seen, hypnosis creates a suggestible mental state and may cause us to believe what we create in our minds is a "reality" that is external to our perceptions and inner beliefs. Similarly, dreams of abuse are not memories, but more likely metaphors for our current life situation at the time of the dream.

When the quality of our future family interactions and our mental and emotional well being is at stake, I believe we must always exercise critical thinking and prudence in making accusations. It is one thing to have a talk with your parent about bad feelings you carry from childhood. It's quite another to have him arrested. And even where there is guilt, I question how can we get to a healing place to feel better about ourselves by opening the door to law-suits, jail time, and public humiliation.

The experience of a false memory is common to all of us. We were mistaken, confused, distracted. We fill in the blanks when we tell of a historical story. I remember it differently than you do. (Loftus, Schachter, Baker, Yapko) If you persist in your version of events and I want to stay on good terms with you, I might begin to think you are right and I am wrong. If you are someone I defer to naturally because of the nature of our relationship (you are an older sibling, an expert, an authority, or have power over me), then I am more likely to revise my memory to match yours. I may rewrite my entire history to conform to your story or theory. I am more prone to revising my history if you deliver your version as fact rather than one of many possible explanations or just your personal version.

No doubt, we all have implanted memories from stories we heard about our childhood. We mixed these stories with memory fragments, photographs, and fantasy to make up a so-called memory that might never have happened. In many ways, this is the stuff of all creativity and art.

I clearly "remembered" staying at my grandparents' home on the day my parents were married even though I wasn't born until eight years later. Since I was often left at my grandparents' when there were major events I was too young to attend, I assumed I was there when my parents married, too. As a small child, it never occurred to me that my grandparents would have missed the wedding too, or that I wasn't born before my parents' marriage.

These alterations of memory and history have come to be called false memory syndrome. It there such a thing? Is there an actual diagnosis by this name? Is it in the Diagnostic and Statistical Manual of Mental Disorders (DSM)? No. But neither is there a real "inner child" or an anatomical location where the unconscious resides. These are all constructs—ways of talking about psychological states and observations of certain behaviors. How we determine what is true or not true is always subject to our theories, our interpretations, and revisions of belief with more facts.

Often, within the context of the process work of therapy, it appears that the objective "truth" of something is less important than what the exploration of the subject evokes. Still, I suggest we use caution and consider the consequences of our assumptions and beliefs if we plan to take action on them. Perhaps we should be less concerned about feeling right—even though it feels so good to be right!

Are there people who have abused others who are hiding behind complaints of false memory syndrome? Undoubtedly.

Each person must sort this out with a willingness to explore his own responsibility, suggestibility, and need for a given outcome.

Carl Sagan in *The Demon-Haunted World*, raises one of the most interesting questions: Both sexual abuse therapists and alien abduction therapists spend months, sometimes years, encouraging their subjects to remember being abused. Their methods are similar and their goals are very similar—to recover painful memories of long ago. In both cases, the therapist believes the patient to be suffering from trauma attendant to an event so terrible that it is repressed. I find it striking that alien abduction therapists find so few cases of sexual abuse and vice versa.

70. Treatment for sexual and physical abuse

People who have suffered from the trauma of sexual and/or physical abuse are most likely to have frequent and intrusive memories of these events. They may be haunted by the memories rather than having repressed them. The experiences interfere with their relationships, their confidence in being a good parent, their feelings about their bodies, and their sexual functioning. They would like to put these memories behind them and move on toward living more productively.

Effectively treating sexual abuse victims requires sensitivity for the client's experience and respect for their interpretation of the events. A client may feel guilty or dirty that this has happened and may feel responsible, as if s/he brought it on or provoked the perpetrator. Therapy will include the reassurance that the offender is responsible for his behavior. The issue will include exploring what is usually a power imbalance in such abuse. The offender may have been a trusted authority figure such as a parent or teacher who has betrayed and manipulated a defenseless child. Children do not have the verbal or cognitive skills to defend themselves or establish and maintain their boundaries as adults do. They may have been taught to be obedient and compliant to the wishes of adults. In fact, it is often the "good" or model child who is the one an offender will choose, knowing that the child will obey his commands to remain silent. Knowing these facts about sexual abuse, the client may be relieved of a lot of the burden of responsibility and shame.

At the same time, the client is encouraged to express some of the rage and grief that he may have suppressed at the time of the abuse in the hope of escaping further mistreatment. Such suppression of feelings will likely lead to a more generalized sense of numbness. The client may feel frozen or numb, particularly in sexual encounters, and be unable to enjoy being in his body in a sensual or sexual way. These frozen feelings can lead to sexual and relationship problems. An awareness that sexual and physical pleasure is normal and not evidence of his being sick can be helpful. If the client received some sexual pleasure during a childhood molestation, that is common and normal. It is not evidence that he provoked the perpetrator.

Much of sexual abuse therapy centers on engaging the client's lost emotional life and encouraging the client to express a whole range of feelings. This is not to wallow in being a victim indefinitely, but to arrive at a realistic perspective of what happened and gain closure on this event. The effective focus is not about blame, but rather on what the client learned from this experience. How can she now view it to make her stronger, more assertive, better equipped to state her limits. Some of the time can be spent on building the skills surrounding boundaries, preferences, and desires and how the client can express them in the context of relationships. The client is encouraged to see this event as only one small part of the many hours of her life and not the defining event. While the abuse was happening, she was also a student, a friend, and had many interests. (Madanes) She can see that this event does not have to ruin her life or her ability to experience healthy and trusting relationships. She can now be aware of her thoughts and feelings and use them as a guide for her future behavior.

Therapists who emphasize the traumatic aspects of abuse and tell clients they will never get over these unhappy events do them a disservice. The suggestion that they will never recover fully from the experience can be a self-fulfilling prophecy, insuring continued treatment.

The client must strike a balance between experiencing the emotions that were not complete at the time and moving on with optimism to a future that is not defined by this event. This is sometimes difficult. How do you know when you've spent enough time expressing your anger and feelings of betrayal? Each person's path to completion and closure will be different and only you can decide what is best for you.

Some of the trend toward seeing oneself as a "victim of child-hood abuse" or even a "survivor of abuse" may keep you stuck rather than facilitating your progress toward full adult, responsi-ble behavior. While effective therapy allows you to experience hurt and acknowledge wounds, it does not keep you stuck in the past and blaming others. Rather, quality therapy helps you to see your strengths and realize your full potential. The rage from your having been mistreated can be re-channeled into productive action to make up for any time you feel you lost and toward being more whole.

In all aspects of therapy, when the focus is on development, improvement, and self-mastery, the client continues to move in those positive directions.

71. Dreams and nightmares

Some therapists use dreamwork as a way to resolve problems in living and inner conflicts. Our dreams come to tell us new information about ourselves. They offer other perspectives on the current issues in our lives. Even when the dream seems to be about incidents from long ago, there is always a current, relevant issue being raised by the dream for the dreamer.

By examining the content of the dream, the feelings, and the layers of meaning, the dreamer can get in touch with lost or denied parts of the self. Often, these are parts of the self that the dreamer projects (in the form of accusations, prejudice, fear, dislike) onto other dream characters, animals, monsters. Dreamwork examines how these elements of the dream are symbols, which represent parts that the person needs to re-own or integrate.

Nightmares, especially recurrent nightmares, seem to tell the dreamer important information that require the dreamer's action or conscious awareness. For nightmares to stop, the dreamer must understand their messages and take action by making changes in his/her life. Just understanding the meaning of the nightmare may not be sufficient for the dream to stop.

The dream is not an accurate representation of reality, but a metaphor for another way of looking at the client's reality. A dream is neither an exact re-enactment of a memory nor a prediction of the future. Instead, it is valuable as a status report in the present, in metaphor, not literal terms, offering more choices in thinking and behavior for the dreamer. When practiced regularly, dreamwork can be a source of inner wisdom and creativity.

In my books, *Dreaming Your Real Self: A Personal Approach to Dream Interpretation* (Perigee/PenguinPutnam, 1998) and *Dream Back Your Life: Transforming Dream Messages into Life Action, A Practical Guide to Dreams, Daydreams, and Fantasies* (Perigee, July 2000), I discuss the variety of dreamwork techniques for working with dreams and nightmares.

Only the dreamer can determine with any certainty what a dream means. Don't allow others to tell you your dreams mean you're mentally ill or to tell you what they mean. Other people's interpretations of your dreams will tell you more about *them* than they will about you.

72. Rituals

Rituals are part of everyone's life, even though we may not recognize what we do as ritual. We shake hands when meeting someone and we celebrate holidays with traditional foods and behaviors. More personally, we might do certain things in a certain way every day, such as having morning coffee, writing in our journals, or kissing family members goodnight.

We perform these daily rituals without much conscious thought about their sequence or style. However, when we don't do them—perhaps while traveling—we miss them. We might feel off-center or foggy without our routine, comforting behaviors. As human beings, we seek patterns and we cling to the familiar ones.

Rituals, however, also speak powerfully to our unconscious. By taking action in words and motion in a ceremony, we engage the senses (with smoke, candlelight, drumming, words). We thereby seem to be able to make a deeper connection to the changes we want to implement than we can by talking about them alone.

To help resolve an old hurt or a psychological wound that seems to fester, you might want to plan a ritual yourself. Decide on the purpose of your ritual (such as saying good-bye to an old way of seeing yourself or welcoming and affirming a positive change). Then determine what actions you want to make this concept and emotional state more concrete. Some typical rituals include burning photos or a piece of paper on which you've written something you want to release (such as an old anger or a belief that no longer serves you), or burying something in the ground, writing a monologue or poem to state your intention and reading it aloud in a suitable setting. Having a witness to your personal ceremony or ritual helps to make it more "real" and facilitates the changes you want to bring about.

Directions for creating personal rituals are in many books on this subject in the bibliography (Mariechild, Hammerschlag, Williamson), and in my book, *Dream Back Your Life.*

73. Role play, psychodrama, and Gestalt therapy

Role play is a technique familiar to many people. It is used in educational as well as psychotherapeutic settings.

Perhaps someone would like to return an item to a store and doesn't know what to say. They might practice this with someone else, having the other person play the part of the store clerk. They may try out different versions, having the "clerk" give different responses that the person would like to be ready for.

Role play can be used for skill-training and practice but is usually not used for deep psychological work, though it can be. For this kind of work where the client examines conflicts and strong emotions, **psychodrama** might be employed. Rather than coming to therapy and only talking about what you'd like to say to someone or wish you had said as an abstract discussion, psychodrama allows the client to act out the scene in the context of a therapy session. Other members of the therapy or psychodrama group can play or stand in for other characters in the drama. The client/protagonist whose drama is enacted will coach the others about how to play their parts. As the drama unfolds, the protagonist, with the guidance of the director, will switch roles, playing each of the other persons and responding as these significant persons to the client's own questions and statements. Since the drama is enacted with props and movement by the participants, the outcome is more than an intellectual understanding of the interplay of personality and psychology. As the protagonist gestures, shouts, weeps, and interacts with the other characters, he has an experience that reaches down into the unconscious in life-changing ways. By engaging all the senses and the full body in the drama, insights and closure can be achieved that might be out of reach from simply talking about problems. In these respects, it resembles a directed ritual.

An additional advantage to psychodrama is that the client can have these conversations and confrontations with people who are either no longer available or inappropriate for such encounters in real life. This could be because one of the significant characters is deceased or because the client fears the consequences of such an encounter in reality, such as being fired by an employer or endangering the health of an elderly and fragile relative.

Psychodrama offers a wide variety of techniques and styles and is a powerful therapeutic method. (Blatner, Dayton, Fox, Sternberg) It can also be very emotional and volatile and should be practiced with people who have the proper training. Clear goals should be formulated before beginning so that the encounter has closure at the end. At the completion of a psychodrama, the client should feel closer to resolution of the concern that brought up the desire for the psychodrama. Frequently, several psychodramas are needed to deal with issues that have many angles and possible approaches. This is especially true when the issue has been haunting the client for a long time.

Gestalt therapy grew out of psychodrama when Fritz Perls studied with J.L. Moreno and then adapted the concepts for his own work. Some of the techniques are similar, encouraging an emotional connection through acting out scenes, creating dialogues with significant others, and making contact through drama and conversation with different parts of the self. Some of these techniques can be practiced alone. An example is the "empty chair" technique where the client plays both sides in a conflict (within himself or with another person) and changes chairs to speak from each part.

74. Brief or solution-focused psychotherapy

Brief psychotherapy is based on the belief that change doesn't have to be always painful, difficult, or take a long time. "Brief" may refer to anything from single-session therapy to as many as twelve sessions over a few months. The goals are specific, limited, realistic, and focused. It avoids elaborate theories and explanations of historical causes without discounting their influence.

This method emphasizes the client's resources and respects the client's knowledge and creativity. It sees the client as an expert on his own problem. The client knows the solution to his problem, even if he doesn't know he knows.

Small successes are celebrated and expanded. The client is instructed to notice what is working in her life and to do more of what works. She is asked to notice when the problem is absent and to capture what goes into that situation so she can expand those skills and behaviors. Since she has probably tried everything that doesn't work, she is asked to do something different. Anything different is likely to be better than more of the same.

Rather than seeing therapy as a quest for some end goal or endpoint of success, therapy is used to get the client "on track," encouraging her to notice all the things she is doing correctly and how she can maintain staying on the right path for her.

The client may also be asked to rate his problem on a scale from 1 to 10, where 1 is the problem at its worst and 10 is the absence of the problem. Where do you rate the problem today? What would you have to do to increase that rating by 1/2 or by 1? How will you know you've improved from a 2 to an 8? This gives the client real measures of his own with standards he has set for himself in observable, action-oriented terms.

Among the techniques frequently used is the Miracle Question by Steven deShazer (1988): "Suppose that one night, while you were asleep, there was a miracle and this problem was solved. How would you know? What would be different?"

This question encourages the client to form a vision of his life without the complaints and problems he has brought to therapy. He is asked to imagine what his life would be like and what he will be doing when his problem is resolved. In many ways, this visioning step sets the goals of the therapy process. It is hopeful and positive and mobilizes the client's ability to make changes.

Solution focused, brief therapy is very helpful for people whose problems are not extensive and who are functioning relatively well in their lives. It may not be as helpful for those who need to make larger changes or who are dealing with problems that need more discussion and emotional release work.

75. Neuro-linguistic Programming (NLP)

The techniques of neuro-linguistic programming could probably be classified with the brief psychotherapies since they are frequently effective in a short period of time. These therapists also remind us all therapy doesn't have to be long, hard, and painful, as many of the more traditional schools of therapy teach. In fact, they say, the expectation of resistance and difficulty sets the stage for unnecessarily prolonging the treatment.

Much of the focus in this method is on how both the client and therapist use language and its influence on thinking styles and beliefs. The therapist investigates how the client perceives his problems or behaviors he wants to change. The emphasis is on mobilizing resources the client already has and being able to vision his life without the difficulties or obstacles he feels he has. Alternate behaviors are explored while honoring the usefulness of past behaviors and experiences. The client is encouraged to use her own creativity to overcome a problem or to generate new ways to behave and react.

If you want to do something you feel you are unable to do, you might imagine someone you know who can do this and copy their behavior. What would Susie do in this situation? Then pretend to be Susie, right down to the nuances of speech and gesture. Practicing the new behavior, you will lose the awkward or artificial feelings.

The concentration is on changing the client's irrational belief systems and erroneous perceptions. How does she conceptualize herself and her world? Emphasis is on the unique observational and representational systems of the client, whether auditory, kinesthetic, or visual, referred to as modalities. For example, some people experience the world more in visual terms and their speech reflects this. They say they see what you are saying or they can picture what you mean. Kinesthetic persons will talk in terms of feelings and how they grasp the ideas. Auditory people are likely to stress whether they've been heard or listened to. They will tell you they hear what you say or tell you what it sounds like to them. Knowing what representational system you use is the beginning of accessing the other systems for greater experience and changing behavior. The therapist can use the client's resources in a particular system while introducing others. (Robbins, Grinder, Bandler, Andreas, Dilts)

The NLP therapist mirrors the client to facilitate rapport. That is, the therapist might match the breathing, speech pace, body language, gestures, and speech patterns to help establish the client's comfort. Techniques include reframing (discussed above), changing perception of time, and imaginal modeling.

You might want to try imaginal modeling on your own. Choose a behavior that you would like to do and is possible for you to do, but you don't feel confident enough to do. Examples are giving a speech, refusing the request of a demanding person, going to a restaurant alone, or making a phone call to ask for information you feel embarrassed about.

Think of someone you know who can do this behavior comfortably. Imagine her doing it. What does she do? What would she say in this situation? How does she conduct herself? In your mind, capture as many details as you can, including her words, actions, and gestures. Then see yourself stepping into that role and doing the same thing. Try it out.

76. Rational-Emotive Therapy (RET)

The focus of this therapy is the client's recognition of how her irrational beliefs, expectations, and demands create uncomfortable or distressing feelings. By examining what the client's beliefs are in any situation, she is able to see how these create her emotions.

No one can *make* you feel bad—even those who may try to. You are the one who puts meaning onto what others say and do. Your expectations or beliefs about how others should behave, think, and feel are what creates your disappointment, anger, hurt, or betrayal. In one way, RET is a structure for reframing. It uses a format of A-B-C-D, where A is the activating event, B is the beliefs about the event, C is the consequence and feelings of your belief, D is disputing your irrational beliefs. (Ellis, Dryden)

After following these steps, the client is then encouraged to experiment with new behaviors, to formulate alternate interpretations of his experiences. He is asked to substitute his irrational beliefs with rational ones. For example, "I must be seen as competent and capable at all times." is changed to "I'd prefer to be seen as competent and capable, but I'm human and it won't kill me if I'm not always seen this way. I can make mistakes sometimes."

Change occurs when the client accesses new choices for thinking and behaving and acts on them. Some therapists give homework so that the client will find herself in an anxiety-provoking situation and discover that nothing really terrible happens, thereby changing the irrational beliefs that cause the unhappy feelings.

Some of the criticisms of RET say that it is heavy-handed and confrontational, but many people affirm its effectiveness. For certain individuals, RET is not the best choice because they have ignored their emotions and need to learn how to focus on their feelings before they can make good choices. They may interpret the work of RET as not being heard or having their emotions trivialized.

As always, the client has to determine what styles and techniques are likely to work best for him or her. Individual therapists, of course, will have different styles of implementing any technique.

77. Breathwork and rebirthing

Some therapies concentrate on the emotions. The belief is that much depression, anxiety, and feeling stuck comes from pent up emotions that have been suppressed or inhibited by the person's environment and beliefs. By expressing these emotions, the client is released from these self- or socially-imposed restrictions. The energy that is used to hold these emotions in check is then freed for other uses: to live more joyfully, to be open to new ideas, to be creative and productive.

Emotional release may be achieved through breathwork, sometimes referred to as rebirthing. The client is asked to breathe deeply and quickly, creating lightheadedness and tingling sensations. Using this form of hyperventilation, the client will enter an altered state (trance), which is supposed to free up emotions ordinarily kept in check by the conscious mind and social constraints. The client may be encouraged to beat pillows, scream and yell, punch a mattress, kick his feet, and say whatever comes to mind. The environment is usually set up for the client's and therapist's protection and privacy with padding, pillows, and soundproofing. The client may find that anger and grief come up and can be expressed. Various schools of psychology may refer to this emotional expression and its accompanying release of tension as catharsis or abreaction.

Bodywork, or deep massage, sometimes creates a similar release. The client may suddenly feel tearful, joyful, or be aware of a nostalgic ache as parts of his body are manipulated, especially if he is told he will. Often, the sudden emotional outbursts created by this work come as a surprise to the client. They may be frightening in their strength, especially if the client is usually contained in his emotional expression. This may cause him to fear he is going crazy or losing control. But such sessions, when conducted by trained and experienced practitioners, are brought to closure. A single therapy session or treatment may last two to three hours. At the end of that time, the client should have returned to his fully conscious and waking state, able to drive and interact normally. He may feel tired and need extra rest. Over time, he will further process the experience, but he should not leave the therapy encounter with his emotions still raw and on the surface. The last part of this work is frequently devoted to re-orienting the client to his surroundings and his plans for the rest of his day so that he can resume his normal functioning.

Because of the volatility of this work and the potential for psychological or physical harm, it is very important that you screen your therapist with the questions suggested earlier in this book. Getting recommendations from others who have worked with someone is also helpful. Especially, ask specifically what you can expect in the treatment. As with choosing any therapist, buyer beware.

78. Sex therapy; Tantric practice

Licensed therapists who take advanced training in sexuality, sexual function, and treatments can be certified to do sex therapy. The requirements and laws vary from state to state. Most therapists, however, will occasionally do sex counseling, making recommendations to clients for handling distress about their sexual desires or performance.

Sexual problems may include concerns about sexual functioning, what is "normal," and what courses of action the client may take to resolve problems. Common concerns brought to therapy are a lack of sexual desire, an inability to stay aroused or maintain an erection, ignorance about how to sexually please a partner, difficulty reaching orgasm and/or ejaculation, or premature ejaculation.

Some people have concerns about the suitability of their sexual desires and seek guidance, validation, and permission for their behavior.

As discussed earlier, whether any behavior is treated as "wrong" or "sick" is culturally determined. In some cultures, cross-dressing (also called transvestitism or wearing the clothes of the opposite gender) or having sexual relations with someone of the same gender is considered one of many ways to be sexual or may even be evidence of contact with the divine. It is neither encouraged or discouraged. In Western culture, both of these behaviors are still not accepted by many people. Therefore, having certain desires causes secrecy, guilt, or an inability to perform sexually in ways that are more "acceptable" to the culture. This forces some people to create their own groups and subcultures.

Much of sex therapy centers on education and giving permission to people to have sex in a way that is most acceptable to them. The emphasis is on responsible behavior with other consenting adults and the necessity for staying within the law. Being aroused by scenes or partners that are not socially acceptable can be the focus of treatment, but may be difficult to change since our sexual behaviors and preferences are imprinted in early life. Genetic influence and the influence of hormones begin before birth in the womb. Your sexual orientation, desires, and preferences are the result of many experiences beginning with those of early life, the expectations of your culture, your body's hormonal functioning, and your beliefs. Sexuality is multi-causal and complex (John Money); it can't be pinned down to a single determinant.

Behavioral therapy might be used to alter sexual patterns that present a problem for the client. These problems are referred to as *paraphilias* in psychological sex literature and some are called *perversions* by the justice system. They include desire for sex with under-age children, the need for violence during sex, and other non-consensual (forced) behavior. Sometimes clients are treated with medication to inhibit desire and behavior that are against the law.

Sex therapy for most people with problems of inhibited desire and arousal may focus on possible causes, but effective treatment usually consists of restoring the natural joy of experiencing the sensations of the body. The therapist might suggest various techniques to be more comfortable with being in your body including massage. She might suggest you masturbate (at home) and experiment with styles of stimulation and satisfaction to discover what you like best. Partners are encouraged to be responsible for their own behavior and needs and to communicate clearly. This includes education about using safer-sex practices, the details of effective birth control, and the risks of any sexual behavior. Sex therapists do *not* ask you to be sexual in their presence.

Tantra is a yogic practice of using sexual energy to enhance intimacy and spiritual connection. It teaches both men and women how to have multiple orgasms with or without a partner. Men can learn how to control ejaculation. Both partners learn techniques to deepen intimacy and commitment and to become more spiritually attuned to one another. Sex is not simply about having an orgasm, but is about feeling more in touch with yourself and your partner. Some Tantric practices include multiple partners, but this is a choice for any individual practitioner. Quality Tantra workshops give participants an opportunity to do or not do any of the suggested exercises. (Anapol, Anand)

79. Constructive Living: Morita and Naikan psychotherapy

Author David K. Reynolds, after studying Japanese styles of psychotherapy, has brought a synthesis of these methods to the West. Rather than calling the troubled person a patient or client, he is called a student. Morita therapists are seen as teachers or educational specialists, giving the student specific strategies for dealing with life.

Morita therapy places its focus on action/behavior in the triangle of thoughts (cognitions), feelings (emotions), behavior (action). He believes most of us spend too much time dwelling on our negative feelings and talking about these feelings. This increases our discomfort and may lead to increasingly painful feelings. He says, rather than trying to change our feelings and thoughts that are not within our control, we can change what is under our control—our behavior. By taking action and moving our large muscles, we are likely to feel better. If we are feeling low and slinking about, we're going to continue to feel low. He says, if we clean the house or wash the car or do something else that needs doing, we will soon begin to feel better. In fact, when we move our bodies, our neurochemistry changes, which then affects our moods—as anyone who exercises knows. In addition, by tackling these chores, we will have done what needs to be done. One might say this is one way to fight analysis paralysis (discussed later).

This is not a Pollyanna psychotherapy nor does it stress "the power of positive thinking" à la Norman Vincent Peale. Rather, it is about taking action and responsibility for one's life, knowing that doing constructive and positive actions builds self-esteem and self-confidence. It emphasizes the mature acceptance of feelings, knowing that feelings come and go and change all the time. In the meanwhile, we do what needs to be done in spite of how we feel—and then feel better for having done it.

The emphasis of *doing what needs to be done* in Morita therapy removes the client/student's self-absorbed, narcissistic preoccupation with problems and worries. By noticing what needs to be done and doing it, he is less likely to get caught up in his problems and less inclined to enlarge them by keeping his attention on them.

Naikan places its focus on contemplating what others have done for us. Rather than encouraging us to complain and moan about our grievances, hurts, wounds, or experience ourselves as a victims of our families and society, Naikan therapy asks us to make note of all that others have done for us. What have they taught us? How many of our meals did our parents prepare or pay for? How many dishes did they wash? How much trouble have we caused others? What have we done to hurt others and cause distress?

We are asked to notice that in doing anything, many other people (some of them unknown to us) have been part of our learning and our ability to accomplish this task. When we are vacuuming, we might think of all the engineers, designers, inventors, and manufacturers that are part of the production of the vacuum cleaner. We become aware of the people who work at the electric company, which makes it possible for us to use this appliance. Who taught us how to clean or use a vacuum cleaner? Who taught us standards for cleanliness and its importance for our health? Who imparted the values of cleanliness and order for aesthetic appreciation of our surroundings? We are encouraged to write thank you notes and to say thank you frequently. We are not asked to feel gratitude since we cannot control our feelings, but we can take the action of saying thank you to our parents and others.

By such meditations and written assignments, we become less engrossed in our suffering and how we are victims. We become able to see ourselves as an integral part of a larger system of humanity and the planet.

Constructive Living is a practical and sensible psychotherapy, especially for those people who talk about feelings to excess and create drama in their lives. It has its correlates in the "here and now" emphasis of Gestalt therapy. Its Eastern flavor combined with its Western, pragmatic slant, appeals to many. Consider this quote from Dr. Reynolds's book, *Playing Ball on Running Water:*

> So don't seek anxiety-free living; don't strive for constant bliss. Choose rather to continue your struggle. Resolve to react forcefully to the challenges of reality. Hold to your goals. Fight your fight. And live with purpose.

However, for people who have spent much of their lives ignoring or numbing their feelings, this therapy might only increase their tendency to distract or repress emotional states. It would seem that this is an effective therapy for those who can identify emotions so they can go on to accept them. But if you don't know what you're feeling or never show your emotions when situations call for their expression, then a more feeling-centered psychotherapy might be more appropriate.

80. Narrative therapy

Each of us has a story of our life. We tell our story more often than we are aware—to ourselves and to others. How we tell our stories, and what we believe about our histories, has made us who and what we are today. It determines how we see ourselves in the future. The story will determine the limits we put on ourselves, who we think we are and what we can do in the future. Our story decides whom we choose to associate with. It tells us how to react and what we can expect of ourselves. Our story tells us whether we are worthy or unworthy of happiness. In total, the stories we tell are how we make meaning of our lives.

Many people who come to psychotherapy feel they have a sad story to tell. They have been mistreated, improperly raised, poorly educated, exploited by others. They sometimes list their sorrows and how they have suffered. They are big on blaming others for their sorrows. Look what happened to me, look what I've become, how I'm a failure, how I suffer—all because of *those people!*

In narrative therapy, the client has an opportunity to tell a different story about her past. This might be another way of reframing. With therapy, the client might see how her struggles and troubles taught her to deal with crises. She might focus on the resources she discovered in herself, her inner powers and strengths. She can emphasize her talents and ability to survive and even triumph in spite of the odds.

"What doesn't kill us makes us strong," as Nietzsche said.

Narrative therapy provides an opportunity to re-write our story rather than accepting the one we've been telling or the one our family told us. A new story offers new possibilities and helps us get unstuck.

81. EMDR

EMDR is an acronym for the system of therapy Eye Movement Desensitization and Reprocessing. It is a relatively recent psychotherapy treatment developed by Francine Shapiro, Ph.D. Using eye movements, tones, or taps, the therapist helps the client to "reprocess" traumatic memories. The neurology behind the rapid changes is still not understood, but Dr. Shapiro speculates that what occurs in the treatment is related to the rapid eye movement (REM) of dreaming, which seems to integrate past and present events. Some dramatic and positive results from this method have been seen in the treatment of Post-Traumatic Stress Disorder (PTSD), which has been particularly intractable to other courses of psychotherapy. In working with Vietnam veterans and other victims of severe trauma such as survivors of earthquakes and the Oklahoma City bombing, therapists have been able to provide rapid relief of symptoms—sometimes after only a few sessions.

Controversy about this method seems to be around the training requirements to call oneself certified. Some therapists state they have used the method successfully simply by reading about it rather than taking training or workshops. Such conflict within the therapeutic community often confuses the issues and can cause us to lose our focus on the patient/client in need of effective treatment at a fair price.

Like all therapies, EMDR incorporates elements from many other models including NLP, other brief psychotherapies, including scaling one's distress from zero to ten. EMDR also incorporates some cognitive therapy by examining the patterns of negative thinking similar to Martin Seligman's three Ps of pessimistic thinking, described earlier—how distress and depression is made worse when it is seen as personal, permanent, and pervasive.

It may be hard to tease out which elements are unique or "revolutionary." And, like any therapy, the techniques and their effectiveness vary considerably with the style and originality of the therapist as well as the receptivity of the client. Some skeptics believe the encouraging results in any therapy have more to do with the enthusiasm and passion of the practitioner than any element of the method. But again, the therapeutic relationship itself and the client's expectations and commitment to change are the most important factors in bringing about positive change, regardless of the belief system or techniques of the therapist.

82. Life skills training

Many times, clients go to mental health professionals because they feel inadequate in certain life situations. Perhaps they are too shy to approach someone for a date or demonstrate extreme timidity in any social situation. Perhaps they are unable to refuse to comply with the requests of others, even when these requests are extremely demanding on their resources of time and money. Others allow themselves to be exploited in job situations or by persuasive salespeople. They are at a loss for what to say. They may feel angry with themselves for not defending their rights or asking questions or maintaining their boundaries.

While these issues frequently come up in psychotherapy, it should be clear to the reader that these are not problems of mental health or illness. The client may simply have never learned the skills to speak clearly and firmly, make requests, ask questions, or refuse politely. The client may lack the skills but not the understanding or inclination to behave in other ways. The focus of the therapy sessions may be on building such life skills or assertiveness training. It may be as basic as making a budget or balancing a checkbook, something the person may never have done before. Others, such as a parent or spouse, have always done these tasks for him. Other life skills include being able to read a map, ask for directions, take notes and study in school or even basic literacy skills such as reading and writing.

It is a common mistake to label someone as sick or mentally ill because she doesn't do what we expect in a social situation. The reason may be that she doesn't know how, not because she is being difficult or hostile. Such assessments are important whether they apply to you or whether you apply them to others.

If you are thinking about seeing a psychotherapist or counselor, you might consider whether your difficulties are due to a lack of skills or caused by being in internal conflict. If it's the former, there are other ways to gain these skills in addition to psychotherapy. Classes and seminars in communication and theater can encourage adults to gain confidence and ease in interacting with others. Role-play and psychodrama also provide skill-building opportunities.

As an example, let us pretend I've purchased an expensive small appliance such as a copy machine. I take it home and discover it isn't working when I set it up. Because it comes with a guarantee, I can return it to the store where I purchased it. But if I am unaccustomed to returning items, this may be cause for great anxiety. I might even prefer to call a repair person and pay to have the copier fixed rather than take it back for repair or request a refund or another copier. By doing a skill-building role-play with a friend or other person I trust, I can try out different ways to express my complaint. My partner in the dialogue can answer in different ways so that I can rehearse possible answers and feel more prepared to take the copier back. She might make suggestions or demonstrate how she would handle it.

While my shyness and reluctance to take the above action might be seen as problems of self-esteem or self-worth, it may also be that I haven't learned the basics of assertiveness skills. I may also not know what my rights are as a consumer—especially if I'm new to this country or have been sheltered by others.

All too often, a lack of skills is treated like a disease, a disorder, or a defect of moral character. The DSM-IV *(Diagnostic and Statistical Manual of Mental Disorders,* the "bible" of diagnosis for mental health practitioners) lists "disorders" of reading, writing, and math skills as diagnostic categories even when the persons—usually children—do not have a learning disability. This makes illnesses out of the ordinary problems of living and learning. Then they need to be treated by the medical profession rather than being accepted and corrected as only deficits in our socialization, child-rearing, and educational systems.

Again, it's important for you, the client, to think clearly about what you need and want when you set your goals in therapy. Other educational or corrective avenues might be more suitable and less costly.

83. Homework and directives

Many schools of psychology use homework, assignments, or directives as part of the therapy. You might be asked to say hello to five strangers by the time of your next session to overcome your shyness. Or your therapist might suggest that for a change, you initiate sex with your spouse or do so at an unusual time. A common homework assignment for couples is to have dinner out together without the children, or to schedule time as a family to discuss concerns and problems. Other frequently used directives are to keep a daily journal or dream journal. Or you may be asked to keep a log of each time you spontaneously do a behavior that you'd like to increase or decrease.

These directives may be given so that the client will practice a new behavior. Other reasons might include the therapist's desire to interrupt an old and ineffective pattern of behavior. Or the therapist might be helping the client to create an opportunity to improve communication and intimacy among family members. Journals and notes the client makes for herself can be helpful to express and unburden uncomfortable feelings. They also help the client to see her own repeating patterns.

Any homework assignments should be offered as suggestions, not as imperatives. The therapist's job is not to take control of your life and tell you what to do. You are the one who should be gaining more control over your own life and having more alternatives to choose from. Those are some of the goals of therapy. Having choices includes choosing what goes on in your therapy. Again, you should be an active participant in your therapy as much as possible. If your therapist suggests homework, feel free to modify it to suit your needs. You might suggest an alternative you think would work better for you. To stretch yourself toward greater progress, you might even want to do something more difficult or demanding than the therapist's suggestion.

Your homework assignments are subject to your approval. You don't have to do anything you don't want to do. For some people, saying no to a therapist is their first step into health. On the other hand, ask yourself how the therapist's directive might be helpful to you.

On rare occasions, I have heard of therapists asking clients to do things that were unethical or against the client's values. I heard of one therapist who was divorcing her husband who was also a therapist. She asked a therapy client to go into her husband's office to steal therapy records. Another wanted to borrow cash from a client to buy a boat. By paying her back with cash income, he could hide money from the IRS. One therapist asked a client to watch his dogs when he was away on vacation. When she attempted to decline, he insisted that it would make her a better, kinder person to do this favor. When she explained how difficult it would be for her to keep the schedule he required for his dogs, he pressured her until she agreed.

These are violations of professional boundaries as well as being against the law.

If you are asked to do anything you believe is wrong, say no. You may want to consult another professional or report the behavior to the licensing board if you believe the request is illegal. This kind of request is not homework. It is exploitation. (See dangers below.) Homework and directives are for your benefit, not your therapist's.

84. What are the possible dangers? Abuses of therapy

Clearly, the examples above are abuses of the therapy relationship. When a therapist uses the power of his position to exert force and control over a client, it is always abuse. This is true even when the therapist believes it is "for your own good." With that kind of authoritarian and dominating attitude, the client may easily be harmed because he is no longer in charge of his life.

Therapy should increase your flexibility and range of choices. It should not imprison you in your therapist's beliefs or make you a follower of her ideas and wishes. When this happens, it is often a re-enactment of the very problems the client came to therapy to resolve—feeling powerless, helpless, and not in charge of his own life. It is the therapist's job to increase freedom, choice, and a sense of mastery and competence in the client. A good therapist does this by encouraging new behaviors and exploring possibilities for alternative actions. The therapist may coach the client in learning the skills needed for improved social interactions and responsible behavior.

If your therapist makes rules for you by telling you what you can or cannot do, what friends to have, what to wear or whom to see, you may consider that your therapy relationship has become abusive. Some serious signs of abuse are discussed below when we look at events that are good reasons to leave your therapist immediately.

85. Are there "crazy" therapies?

Some therapies are "crazy" therapies. Any therapy can turn crazy when it becomes dogmatic or focused on a single way of looking at problems. We already examined some beliefs about alien abduction or childhood abuse that can create more problems in the client than he had when he started therapy. Other "treatments" include exorcism (the removal of evil spirits through religious rituals), the use of magic and charms, prophecy and psychic readings, and fortune telling. These kinds of indoctrination have all the markers of classic mind control techniques and are not accepted as standard practice among mental health professionals and licensing boards. They have nothing to do with solving the problems that people bring to therapy.

In my opinion, they rob the client of the opportunity for critical thinking and the freedom to make up her own mind about what happened to her and what will happen to her in the future. As we have seen, some so-called therapies judge the ordinary problems and frustrations of living as being evidence of a mental disorder or disease. I have heard of women who were hospitalized and remained apart from their husbands and children for months because they were "too attached." Some therapists label the client's interests, pleasures, and passions as "addictions." They automatically see abuse in family nudity and frank discussions. They encourage the mindset of "victimology" that removes our freedom to choose how we react to any situation, whether traumatic or not.

Many therapies are innovative and pioneering, but they may also be untested with no track record of proven effectiveness. If something in your therapy seems a bit "crazy" to you, you might consider checking it out. Ask someone else whose opinion you trust what they think of what is giving you cause for concern. You might call a local university and ask to talk to someone who teaches in the psychology department to get another point of view.

86. When your personal belief system is judged as "crazy"

You may hold beliefs that your therapist considers "crazy." For example, one person's religious beliefs may be superstition to the next person. How do you know if his assessment of you is correct? Maybe this is just a conflict in belief systems and your therapist isn't being respectful of your right to understand the world differently. After all, who should decide what's crazy about anything? As noted, mental wellness or illness is culturally determined.

But these disagreements can be passionate and troubling. Wars are fought over conflicting religions and cosmologies, with each side demonizing the other. If you hold a belief and go to therapy to work on some problem that is unrelated to the way you believe the universe works, you may want to discuss your goals with your therapist. If he has redefined the goals in a way that you feel is unhelpful or is unnecessarily derailing you from what you want to accomplish, get another opinion. Or get another therapist.

87. Getting another opinion

As with any professional service or product, there are many varieties, strategies, and points of view. Your therapist should take your doubts and concerns seriously. If you feel you are at an impasse, you might want to consult someone else. An appointment with another professional *not recommended by the therapist you are seeing* may be helpful.

If you wanted to patch your roof and the roofer told you that you needed a whole new roof, you would probably ask one or two other professionals for their opinions before proceeding. If you went to a dentist for a cracked filling and he told you needed extensive dental work unrelated to the filling, you would be likely to ask the opinion of another dentist.

Take the same kind of care with your mind and your future mental health. You are the expert on your problems and what is good for you. You have known yourself longer and better than your therapist has known you. No matter how much therapists behave as if they know what is better for others, they usually don't.

Because new psychological techniques and new ideas of how to deal with problems are being explored all the time, many of them are untested and untestable. Don't let a therapist who speaks with great confidence and authority intimidate you into denying your own hesitancy and caution.

If you have a doubt, check it out. You can call a psychology department at a local college or university and ask questions. You can also call local clinics or mental health services. You can speak to someone in social services at a local hospital. Try calling a psychiatric facility and ask to speak to a physician. Your Yellow Pages will have many possible sources of information if you have questions. You can even call the licensing board for your state and ask for information about the law and ethical standards for these issues.

Ask questions! You will, at the very least, learn how many different answers you can get to the same question. This will encourage you to think on your own and determine what makes sense to you.

88. The "One True Path"—gurus and megalomaniacs

Some therapists come to their work with a single world view or a single school of psychological thought. This, by definition, puts the client at risk for having fewer rather than more choices as a result of her therapy. If the therapist thinks there's only one path to "get it right," that one may be unsuited to your needs or your personality style.

More dangerous, though, are those therapists who come to see themselves as saviors, gurus, or other enlightened beings. They may hold fantasies of changing the course of history. They may want to change the world and make all people loving and kind. They may believe that through their personal psychological system, humanity will be changed forever and they will have immortality—metaphorically or literally.

Perhaps gurus are in part created by the seductive climate of a steady stream of devoted clients who admire, praise, and tell the therapist how much he has helped them. The therapist, caught up in the wave of self-inflation and glory, may forget she is human and therefore imperfect and flawed, just as her clients are. He may believe a therapy that worked extremely well with one or two persons or with himself is now the solution to all the world's problems. She believes she has found the magic key to happiness and peace of mind for everyone.

It is unfortunate that fame and recognition for work well done seem to encourage this kind of ego inflation and the dangers that go with it. The therapist may no longer proceed cautiously or take feedback from colleagues. She may develop more and more methods that border on the dangerous and exploitative. Or she may become demanding and punishing of those who disagree or who object to the violation of their client rights. Some have become physically abusive to their clients and staff. (See the case of Dr. John Rosen in Richard Ofshe's *Making Monsters* and other examples in Margaret Singer's *"Crazy" Therapies*.)

If a therapist, or anyone else for that matter, insists she has found the One True Path, I suggest you remind her that the path may be perfect for *her*, but cannot be perfect for everyone because people are different.

Success with one individual may be just a fluke or a coincidence. It doesn't mean the system will work with others or could even be repeated with the same client on a different day. Therapy is not an exact science; it is more of an art. Even for experienced therapists, sometimes it's just hit and miss. Several strategies may be tried before one resonates or works with a particular client. That is why the best therapists have a variety of techniques, suggestions, and styles of working, thereby adapting to each client's needs.

It is unfortunate and instructive that many of the big names in psychotherapy became caught up with extravagant and dogmatic claims as their fame and fortune grew. Opening institutes in their names seems to be one indication of seeing themselves as geniuses and gurus. Many of these revered leaders of psychology were later exposed to be less than pure in their motives and methods. Jeffrey Moussaieff Masson, in *Against Therapy* shows us how this is true, to a certain extent, of all the "greats": Sigmund Freud, Carl Jung, Fritz Perls, Carl Rogers, and others.

Even today, much of the criticism from one school of therapy toward those in another implies a "one true path" mentality. You as the consumer, need to be wary of signs of self-inflation in your therapist, especially if he or she has achieved some public recognition and has become well known. Your pathway to health and wholeness must be your own, not one assigned to you by a charismatic therapist with delusions of grandeur. Sometimes the evidence for a therapist seeing herself as a guru is more obvious in a group setting. We'll look at the warning signs later.

89. How do you feel after your sessions? How do you feel about your therapist?

Many studies have shown that one of the most therapeutic aspects of psychotherapy is the relationship between client and therapist. As noted, this may be the first time you have ever had someone listen to you with caring, kindness, and respect. It may be the first time your point of view and your feelings have been taken seriously. This, alone, is healing and encourages the client to trust his/her own reactions and judgment. The client begins, more frequently, to look within for wisdom and guidance.

Your experience of your therapy sessions should, overall, make you feel better about yourself and your therapist. This is not to say that you will come out of every session feeling better. Sometimes you will hate the process or feel bad about what you discover about yourself and your need to change and be more responsible. Sometimes you will feel pained by coming to terms with stressful reality. But overall, your sessions should show an upward trend of improved self-confidence, self-respect and a sense of respect from the therapist. But if, overall, you consistently feel worse after your sessions, if your depression or anxiety is increasing, if your relationships are deteriorating and your symptoms are intensifying, then something is not right. You are in therapy to get better, not worse. If you feel worse, your therapy may be making you worse.

Similarly, if you find that you dislike your therapist, distrust him, or feel put-down or abused in any way, this must be addressed at once. This may be a gradual process as you get to know your therapist and she reveals herself in what she says over time. Your feelings toward your therapist are important, especially because of the transference. Your feelings toward the therapist need to be addressed as they come up or they will be an obstacle to your progress. If your feelings toward your therapist cannot be resolved to your satisfaction, then it may be time to move on to another therapist. A responsible therapist may suggest this. Or perhaps it is time for you to continue your inner work on your own.

The problem with making this decision is that people frequently want to and do quit therapy just as they are getting to the issues that offer the most potential for growth and positive change. These are also the ones that cause the greatest upheaval in emotions and mood and it's this discomfort that makes clients want to flee.

For example, if, in the therapy, I become aware of my being less honest than I believe myself to be, this is a contradiction of my self-image and can be very upsetting. I might feel as if I'm being persecuted or falsely accused by the therapist and may want to quit the therapy to get away from these feelings and my "accuser." When I quit therapy to avoid this discomfort, I miss the growth opportunity to see the discrepancy between my ideal self and my real self. As a human being, I am not perfect. What do I want to do about this sort of "dishonesty" that I've discovered?

It is important to examine what has brought up your negative feelings about your therapy or your therapist before acting impulsively and making an abrupt end to the therapy. This may be a good time to consult with someone close to you whom you trust to get another point of view. Seeing our character defects is never easy or pleasant, but someone who cares for us can help us see ourselves to foster our growth.

90. Trust and safety; therapy as a safe place

Related to how you feel during and after your sessions are the important issues of trust and safety. Trust is connected with other issues we discussed earlier such as privacy and confidentiality. It is also about feeling confident that you will be treated with respect and caring. Trust contains the assumption that your therapist primarily has your best interest at heart, not his own— even at times when it interferes with his own preferences or beliefs. Such occasions might come up in scheduling sessions or if you are in crisis and in need of some support by telephone or to have an emergency session. But such trust in her goodness and kindness usually extends to the reliance that she will be helpful and have the means (compassion, education, and training) to be helpful with your particular set of problems and concerns.

Trust includes an expectation that you will get better and no longer need the therapist. You expect that the therapist will "do no harm," and that she will encourage you to make it on your own instead of feeling more needy and dependent on her.

All of this is about feeling safe. The therapist provides a safe space where you are free to explore your innermost feelings and thoughts, your behavior, history, and hopes for the future. This means feeling not only physically safe with the confidence you won't be struck or hit by your therapist no matter what you say or do, but also psychologically safe. You have confidence that you will not be ridiculed, trivialized, condemned, or humiliated in any way. You have every right to expect to be treated with honor, care, empathy, kindness, and fairness.

Should you feel the therapist has done anything that falls into the category of contempt, derision, sarcasm, or disdain, *say so immediately*. Say what you feel and make sure this is addressed. Allow time for clarification and change. If you then feel your therapist continues being cruel in any of these ways, your therapy is no longer a *safe space* and it's time to make an exit.

One woman went to see a male therapist with her husband because of a marital problem. She had made the appointment and at the beginning of their first conjoint session, she explained what was troubling her in the relationship with her husband. She had spoken only a few sentences when the therapist turned to the husband and said, "Is she always like this?"

The woman had the good sense not to schedule another session with this therapist.

91. When therapy shrinks the Self; Therapist as "expander"

Throughout this book, I have emphasized how therapy should increase your choices and alternatives; it should result in your being more flexible in your behavior. Michael Hoyt (1995) points out how we have come to use the word "shrink" to refer to psychotherapists and psychiatrists. He says this reveals the fears many people have that the therapy will somehow make them smaller and less than what they were when they started therapy. They will be brought down to size, shrunk to acceptable proportions, confined to social limitations. He makes a point of telling his clients that the purpose of therapy is to expand their range of behavior and have a wider latitude of responses and reactions. Choices are increased by therapy. He sees himself as an "expander" rather than a "shrink."

Therapy, at its best, expands the self in the direction of its full potential. It does not shrink it.

In the course of your sessions, do you feel as if your choices are increasing? Do you feel more possibilities have opened up to you? Are you discovering more resources and abilities you didn't know you had before therapy?

If you can answer yes to these questions, then you don't have to worry about being "shrunk."

92. When the therapist tries to remake you in his/her own image

We have talked about how some therapists get too enamoured of being affirmed and adored by their clients.

Some therapists also come to believe they have found THE ANSWER to living happily and fully. They want others to experience the same joy. They may believe the only way to do that is for their clients to follow the same path as theirs. Therefore, they encourage their clients to make the same life choices they have: "You, too, will be happy if you marry wisely, have two lovely children, and buy a house in an upscale neighborhood." Since many people believe this is the only path to health and happiness, the client is tempted to emulate a therapist who seems to have achieved this American dream. The influence is even more powerful when the therapist holds himself up as a model of mental health and achievement. Invariably, the client is back in his child-like role of wanting to imitate the idealized parent and be just like mommy or daddy. Such a set-up infantilizes the client.

Unfortunately, this never works. It doesn't work with your biological family because you discover your parents are all too human and flawed. And it can't work in therapy for the same reason. Additionally, it is the purpose of therapy for you to find your own path and your own bliss—whatever they may be. Your getting on track toward fulfilling your potential and expanding your choices will evolve in your own way. Your path is not a carbon copy of someone else's, not even your therapist's. Especially not your therapist's. This is notably true when you discover, as many people do in therapy, that your path is not mainstream, traditional, or what others told you they thought it "should" be for you.

Perhaps some of your struggle has been with the discovery of your not being like everyone else. Therapy is about discovering that no one is. While we share a common ground of humanity and human strivings, we each accomplish these in our own unique way.

Likewise, if you hold conservative, traditional values and are not trying to change them, it is not the therapist's place to shame you into changing them to be more modern.

Your therapist can be a role model for you in many ways by helping you to explore other ways to react, take risks and initiative, assert yourself with respect for the rights and feelings of others. She may demonstrate some of these choices. However, her job is not to make you over in her own image. If you feel your therapist is putting pressure on you to make life choices that match his or hers, it is again time to ask questions and reevaluate your therapy.

93. Therapy as "a cell of revolution"

When people come to therapy, they are in distress. Frequently, they are feeling anxious and depressed about what they see in the television news and in their neighborhoods: poverty, war, inadequate housing and healthcare, violence, homelessness, declining educational standards, ecological disasters, corporate crime, religious wars, corrupt governments, incurable diseases. They express their feelings of hopelessness and wonder how they can find peace and meaning in their lives against this backdrop of despair and so many circumstances that seem out of their control.

Traditionally, therapy's focus has been on how these issues reflect more personal concerns. Perhaps the client is dealing with his guilt over being materially comfortable while others suffer and do without. Perhaps his distress comes from an awareness of his own mortality. Saying that the world is falling apart may be a metaphor for the client's feelings that he is falling apart.

But that is only one layer. As some of us learned in the 70s, the personal is political. Each one of us who votes can have an impact on our government. We can send faxes, write letters, make phone calls, and send telegrams to affect laws and social change. Perhaps more importantly, one at a time, in our relationships most close to us, in our families and communities, we can change the way people treat one another by starting with the way we treat others and expect to be treated by others.

James Hillman, in *We've Had a Hundred Years of Psychotherapy and the World's Getting Worse* (Hillman and Ventura, 1992), suggests that therapy is a cell of revolution. It can be a place where the client takes responsibility for being a member of society instead of seeing his concerns only narcissistically. When therapy focuses on the social issues, it is an opportunity for the client to step into the larger community by seeing oneself a part of it and having agency or power in it. In doing so, this lends the meaning to life that so many people feel is absent.

In the past, therapy was often used as a vehicle of social control and conformity. People were expected to adjust, to come to terms with their circumstances. If a man was unhappy that he worked too many hours and had no time for his private or family life, he was reminded of his role as breadwinner and head of household. If a woman described her frustrations with the boredom of housekeeping, of not using her talents and education, she was expected to conform to her role as dutiful wife and mother. They were told their neuroses prevented them from accepting their destiny. Similar messages were given to homosexuals who were also once treated as being mentally ill and sometimes still are.

Therapy was (and sometimes still is) a place where the distress people felt was labeled as *only* their problem instead of a partial product of living in the context of social problems and the deteriorating social supports of community. The problems include sexism, racism, and an economic system that sometimes discourages creativity, individuality, and personal fulfillment.

Hillman reminds us that therapy can be a place where it is safe for clients to express their distress at social problems and not just how they are affected personally or emotionally. It can be a place where the client is spurred to action to do her part to make a better world, starting with how she treats and views herself and her everyday contacts.

94. Judging your progress

In the course of your therapy, you will wonder at times whether it is helpful or whether it continues to be helpful. You may wonder how you can know if you are making progress, going backwards, or just spinning your wheels. Maybe you need some time to assimilate your progress to date.

If you have set some clear goals at the start of your therapy and revised them as you proceed, you will have some way to measure your progress. Have you overcome your fears in certain social situations? Are you able to "feel the fear and do it anyway," as Susan Jeffers says it? Have you made the kinds of changes you hoped for? In general, are you feeling better about your life and about yourself?

Progress in psychotherapy results in some or all of the following: increased choices, increased self-confidence, a willingness to accept calculated risks, the ability to accept ambiguity and uncertainty, being kind to yourself and others, improved communication and assertiveness, the ability to speak your truth clearly and with respect for others, being true to yourself, accepting the reality that you and others aren't perfect, tolerating and even celebrating the differences in others, acting responsibly and ethically, knowing what is right for you and no longer seeking all your approval outside yourself.

In addition, progress may be measured by your increased sense of living more joyfully and spontaneously. Rather than having a rulebook or a set of guidelines to be "healthy," you are likely to experience more happiness in the simple things of life. The ordinary can become an occasion for pleasure and even bliss. You are likely to be more satisfied with what you have and who you are now instead of waiting for something you don't have now to bring you happiness in the future.

When a client in therapy wants to discuss her progress with her therapist, it is quite reasonable to ask for some time to do this. If you have doubts about whether your therapy is helpful or is continuing to be beneficial, it is your responsibility to bring this up in your sessions. You may have gone as far as you can go with this therapist. Or your therapist may be ill equipped to deal with the issues of concern to you now.

In any case, assess your progress frequently, just as you do in any other part of your life.

95. Analysis paralysis

Sometimes, therapy becomes a setting where the client attempts to discuss and analyze everything in his life. He doesn't make any decisions or definitive choices without discussing them with the therapist. He puts his life on hold until he is "better" or knows more about himself or is "healed." He wants to wait to do anything different until he feels better.

The client is in limbo—unable to take action because any action surely has some neurotic motivation, which must be eradicated before taking a step. The client waits. She doesn't commit to a plan; perhaps she doesn't make one. She is waiting for the right time, until she has all the facts.

Perhaps she is waiting for the therapist to tell her she is on her own.

Some therapists encourage this limbo state, actually asserting that clients in therapy shouldn't change jobs or get divorced or make any other major decisions until they have analyzed every aspect of the issue. Caution in making important decisions is wise and it is certainly prudent to give these choices considerable thought, but the therapy shouldn't become an excuse for inertia and inaction in all spheres of your life. This can contribute to reliance and dependence on the therapist until the client becomes unable to think independently.

This analysis paralysis, as I like to think of it, is unfortunate. It robs the client of the power of varied experience and learning from mistakes. When you put off doing what you fear or avoid being in those situations that cause you anxiety, you are missing the opportunity to practice your skills and learn what you can about yourself with the assistance of the therapist. If you wait until after you're "done" you will find *there is no such thing as "done."* Nor is there such as thing as "cured." Learning and growing is a lifelong process.

The advantage of taking risks while you're in therapy is that you have the therapist's encouragement and support as well as some honest, compassionate feedback that you might not receive from others when you blunder. Together, you can turn over your various choices and how you made them or handled them and learn about how you interact with the world. With some coaching, you can explore ways to interact more effectively.

But therapy is not a place to retreat while you're waiting to learn to "get it right." Therapists who encourage this idea in their clients are stunting their growth and inappropriately controlling their clients' lives as well as capitalizing on a possibly endless therapy for their own economic advantage.

96. Dependence vs. autonomy and freedom

Ultimately, the goal of therapy is for the client to feel a greater sense of freedom and autonomy. Too often, as we've seen, clients come to rely on the therapist or the therapy hour to do their serious thinking and inner work. The client looks to the therapist for continued guidance and help in being reflective or in contemplating his choices. He "saves" his psychological work for his therapy sessions.

Over time, the client can become more and more dependant on the therapist for this personal attention and help. As his dependency grows, the client feels, at some level of his consciousness, more helpless and unable to cope. Instead of taking the tools of personal growth with him, he uses them only at the therapist's office.

Such dependency is normal as long as it is short-lived and recognized for what it is: a retreat from adulthood into a child-like role where the therapist is the good, protective parent. But a truly good therapist discourages this dependency and repeatedly puts the responsibility for the client's life and her psychological work back on her.

Therapy is about being autonomous and free, not trading one set of constraints and restrictions for another. In productive therapy, the client will feel a greater sense of freedom and choice. He will feel capable and competent to make choices wisely and to handle their outcomes, whatever they may be. And he will be able to do this without being coached and prodded by the therapist indefinitely.

97. Making your own decisions and choices

As we have seen throughout this book, much of what you learn in therapy is that you have more choices than you thought you did. Frequently, the responsibility of making those choices, especially important ones, feels like a burden. A client who has been used to having others make his choices, even when he also complains about being controlled by others, might have a hard time making his own decisions. When you make your own decisions, you have no one else to blame if the outcome is unsatisfactory. If you've made an error in judgment, you can no longer say that someone else "made" you do it.

The client's usual temptation is to put the therapist in the role of his decision-maker. Client's will ask, "Should I get a divorce?" "Should I go back to school?" "Should I quit this job I hate?"

These are important decisions. To be a fully autonomous adult, we each need to make our own choices and be ready to deal with the consequences. Successful therapy is not a promise of worry-free or problem-free living. You just learn to handle more and see that you have a wider menu to pick from.

But ultimately, the choices are yours. Any therapist who is willing to take on the responsibility for your choices by telling you what to do—no matter how much you long for him to do so—has violated your boundaries and is keeping you a child.

98. Isolation and attachment

Clients get attached to their therapists. This is expected and is part of the positive transference, a natural outcome of good rapport and liking your therapist. Moreover, because a good therapist will contribute to you feeling better about yourself, you are likely to value this relationship above many others. It has been said that we love people because of how we feel about *ourselves* when we are with them more than because of how we feel about *them*. Therapy is a prime example of this axiom since we usually know little about our therapists and spend a lot of time focused on ourselves.

The attachment is normal and positive but can become problematic if it leads to isolation in terms of your other relationships. If what you have with your therapist is your only relationship, then your therapy is not helping you to live in the world with others and get along with other people. If your therapist consistently discourages your other relationships, finds fault with them, or otherwise isolates you from others, you may want to address this as a potential problem with your therapy. Having relationships with others is part of having choice and freedom. These contacts are opportunities to learn to be more open, authentic, respectful of others and of yourself. As you talk about your encounters in the world with others, you will offer material to further your growth in your therapy sessions.

Yes, it is helpful to have an attachment to your therapist, because the relationship of caring, trust, and being able to be yourself with the therapist is what makes therapy work. But if this relationship is your only attachment, it is not good for your mental health because your world has become narrower and restricted, not wider. It also gives an unscrupulous and unethical therapist an occasion to control you for his own needs.

Make sure to cultivate and nurture your other attachments—new and old—while you are in therapy so that you don't become isolated, with your therapist as your only confidante or emotional support. In general, your other relationships should improve and be more satisfying as you learn from your therapy experience.

99. Diagnosis and being a patient

Many people believe that a diagnosis is a "real" evaluation of a person, that the diagnosis is a real category that a person either fits or doesn't fit. In fact, diagnoses, like other psychological entities such as your "inner child" are just ways to talk about problems. Being assigned a diagnosis doesn't mean it's correct. Nor does it mean there is now a clear course of treatment based on the diagnosis. In medicine, a diagnosis is often reassuring because you think that if the doctor has a name for your illness, he will then know what to do for it to help you get better. That's frequently not so in medicine and it's less so in the field of mental health. In fact, the medical model of diagnosis generally points toward pathology: what's "sick" or "wrong" with someone rather than looking at strengths and abilities that need to be encouraged and expanded.

In general, I don't like to use diagnoses. Certainly, they have their place in filing insurance claims since the therapist must assign a diagnostic category with its DSM code number in order for insurance to pay for the therapy. But for the client, this can be more than unhelpful. Many people identify with this label instead of seeing it as a descriptive term for a temporary state. They become the diagnostic category. They might say, "I'm bipolar;" or "I'm OCD" or "I'm a chronic depressive."

This can keep people stuck in their problems. They not only *have* a problem; they *are* the problem. The diagnosis is not simply a behavior they manifest, but an identity. They become problem-focused instead of solution-focused. They see themselves as fixed or determined instead of just dealing with a bump in the road on the journey of life.

In many ways, diagnosis can be just a fancy way of calling people names. Soon they start to call themselves these names. Diagnoses seem to encourage the victim mentality. Stephen Covey says, "Argue for your weakness and it's yours." I believe diagnosis encourages that. Most people already feel bad about themselves because they've been called names and have been criticized all their lives. Therapy shouldn't repeat this trauma.

Similarly, being a "patient" has all the medical implications that come with it. The patient is the one who is sick—mentally sick. It implies something wrong at the core of the person and makes it difficult for the person to see herself as someone with a transitory problem she can overcome or discard. This sense of being a patient can add to feelings of helplessness and hopelessness and lower self-esteem.

Conversely, some of our characteristics need to be accepted rather than corrected, as Martin Seligman says so well in *What You Can Change…And What You Can't*. Language is important. The terms we use indicate hierarchy and power, as with the words "shrink" versus "expander." Using the term "client" implies a more egalitarian condition than the word "patient." How you think and feel about yourself and the words you use will have an impact on how you use your therapy. You can make progress or go backward into a more childlike and dependent state. Being aware of these language choices can be helpful because it is part of the story you tell of who and what you are.

100. Medication

Some psychotherapists are psychiatrists, who are also medical doctors. They are licensed to prescribe medication, including psychoactive drugs to treat certain kinds of mental disorders. There are also psychiatrists who are strictly psychopharmacologists and dispense medication without doing psychotherapy. Some of the disorders likely to be treated with medication are depression, hallucinations (sensing things that are not present or not sensing things that are present), and overwhelming anxiety, perhaps in the form of panic attacks. Various medications seem to fall in and out of favor and usage as we learn more about them. Witness the stardom of Valium and Prozac.

Medication can be helpful, especially when used in the short term to give the person a "window of opportunity" to experience what life is like without some of the debilitating and distressing effects of chronic symptoms. (Kramer, 1993) Without the intense anxiety clouding his thinking, a client may be able to experience what it feels like to live in the world and be with others in a more relaxed state. He may thereby be better able to access this state naturally without medication in the future.

The pharmaceutical industry is big business with the potential for huge profits if their drugs become accepted and frequently used. Peter Breggin (1992) points out that the drug companies sponsor conferences for the American Psychiatric Association (APA) and also fund drug studies. They encourage doctors to give away the free samples they offer. Surely, this constitutes a conflict of interest. How can critical, objective research—as hard as that is anyway—be accomplished when the organization footing the bill for the study has a stake in a particular outcome? We have all heard of companies that withheld information that would have potentially offered protection or warnings to the consumer. These have been especially obvious in products such as cigarettes and dangerous cars. I expect there will be more of these exposes about pharmaceuticals in the future, including some of the most widely used drugs on the market today.

As consumers, it is important to understand some of the reasons why medication is so easily dispensed in the psychiatric community. As we have seen, psychotherapy, a talking therapy, takes time, skill, and training. It requires patience, sensitivity, and an ability to respect the client even when the content of what he says may be offensive or repulsive to the therapist. Therapists who work with clients in order to help increase the clients' skills at solving their own problems are taking the harder road, though perhaps the more enduring one. Talking therapy and teaching techniques for problem solving take longer and usually require more thought than writing prescriptions.

The client wants relief and the doctor who writes a prescription promises quick deliverance from the patient's distress. But it is like giving the proverbial hungry man a fish instead of teaching him to fish. Do we want a nation or a world of people who take drugs to deal with their unhappiness and distressing emotions? How different is this from the person who takes cocaine or shoots up heroin to dull his emotional pain? How about the person who uses alcohol to drown his sorrows? Does the legality of the drug make it more mentally healthy?

Medications may have as much potential for harm as they have for help. You, as the consumer of a medication must take responsibility for your own health. Notice how you feel about the prospect of taking a medication, perhaps indefinitely. Ask questions and take the initiative to request changes if you think a medication is not working for you. If you are built small or are very sensitive to medications generally, you might suggest taking a lesser dosage as a start than the amount recommended for adults weighing 150 pounds or more.

Before taking any medication, ask your doctor the following questions: Why do you think this drug will help me? What is the generic name for this drug? How long has it been in use? Or how long since FDA approval? What are the side effects? What are the effects of taking this drug with the other medication(s) I now use? (Your doctor may not know what other drugs you are on and these may be dangerous when taken in combination. You must be responsible to let your doctor know about your other medications.) How long do you expect that I will be taking this medication? Is it habit-forming or addictive? What can I expect to happen if I discontinue taking it? You might even want to look up the drug in the latest edition of the PDR (Physician's Desk Reference) at the library or your local bookstore. Your health is at stake and some side effects can be long lasting or permanent.

Ask questions. Be an informed consumer.

101. Electroconvulsive therapy (ECT or shock therapy)

Shock therapy, also called electroconvulsive therapy or ECT, uses a current of electricity passed through the brain to produce unconsciousness and convulsions. Many people believe shock treatment is no longer in use, but there has been an increase in its use in recent years. Generally, it is used in hospital settings for the treatment of depression, but is now being used more widely by psychiatrists in private practice. The treatment has often been considered a last alternative when drug therapy doesn't work in severe depression, especially among the elderly, and particularly elderly women. But some doctors use shock as their treatment of choice.

Medical evidence and years of study indicate that ECT causes brain damage. The patient commonly awakens from this treatment dazed, confused, fearful, and with memory loss. Additionally, she may experience nausea, a stiff neck, and headache. Convulsions produced by the shock can be sufficient to cause physical injuries such as broken bones. Depression may appear to be alleviated temporarily, but killing brain cells is certainly a harmful way to address someone's emotional distress. People who are encouraged to submit to ECT are often not fully informed of the risk of death or of the long-term negative effects this treatment creates. Many doctors who use ECT and drugs frequently do not address the social and psychological issues of these depressed patients nor do they offer them other choices to improve their lives. Many would be helped greatly by participating in the many alternatives to therapy and medical interventions that are listed later in this book.

While the dangers of shock to the psychiatric patient are many, the benefits to the doctor administering this "treatment" probably account for its widespread use. Doctors can see many patients at lucrative rates for simply pushing a button. At several hundred dollars a shot, this is more time-effective for the doctor than listening and problem solving with a patient for a full session at a lower fee.

I questioned one psychiatrist about why he no longer used shock therapy. He said that he used to do it at a local hospital in the operating rooms, but since these had to be used very early in the morning, he stopped using this treatment. He said he was a night person and didn't like getting up that early. He made no mention of considering the benefit or hazard for the patients.

Peter Breggin (1992) demonstrates how shock treatment can be an expression of the doctor's hostility toward his patients. In speaking to a patient's husband, one doctor referred to the treatment as a "mental spanking" for a his wife.

Should your doctor recommend shock treatment for your depression, you would do well to consult other therapists who use non-damaging but effective methods to treat depression at its roots.

102. Hospitalization

Psychotherapy clients are sometimes hospitalized for treatment. Hospitalization can help by temporarily removing the client from a situation at home or at work that is significantly detrimental to his getting well. By placing the client in new surroundings, many of the outside causes of his behavior can be eliminated. This is especially true for people who want to be treated for drug or alcohol addiction where the triggers for use of the chemicals may be family strife, the encouragement of peers, or certain kinds of stress. Out of the usual environment, the client has an opportunity to examine his feelings and abilities to manage them without the overwhelming experience of anxiety that may be part of his daily life.

In-patient treatment programs for substance abuse are in the four-week range, allowing the first two weeks for detoxification. The second two weeks (or more) help get the client *on track* toward more effective ways of dealing with his emotions. Instead of using alcohol or other drugs to smother the uncomfortable feelings, the client learns to express them in the hospital setting in both group and individual counseling. He gets to interact with others struggling with the same issues and observes a variety of other responses to his emotions and difficulties.

Hospitalization is also used for clients who pose a danger to themselves or others. The threat of suicide or homicide can precipitate an involuntary hospitalization. Most states require a therapist or other professional to take action to prevent violence when they know the client is seriously contemplating hurting herself or others. In these cases, the client can be hospitalized against her will even if she recants the threat and says she wasn't serious.

It is important to recognize that hospitalization is sometimes used by family members and professionals to incarcerate "difficult" people who do not conform to the desires and expectations of others. Many people have been hospitalized for years when family members have been willing to say that the person was dangerous. With the benefits paid by Medicare, many mental health facilities are exploiting the economic opportunity to hold elderly clients who are neither dangerous nor mentally ill. Many of these facilities simply house these elderly people who receive neither therapy nor assistance in improving their mood or life skills. They may be shocked and otherwise mistreated under the guise of "therapy" and then deteriorate mentally and emotionally, thereby "confirming" the original diagnosis. This is a profitable enterprise for the mental health facility, but in a country that prides itself on human rights, this is an outrage.

Before you agree to be hospitalized or to participate in having someone hospitalized, find out what the facility offers and how this will be of benefit. Elderly people will frequently do better with hiring someone for individual care in the home and at a much lower cost. The potential for abuse in medical care is enormous, particularly when it comes to treating those who may have difficulty expressing themselves, such as the elderly and children, and those with difficulty in reasoning. To conclude these people are mentally ill is to do them a disservice that may have permanent repercussions.

103. How much therapy is enough? When are you done?

Many clients want to know how long therapy will take. How do you know when you are done? How do you know when it's time to stop seeing your therapist? Who decides?

Psychotherapy can vary from a single session (called Single Session Therapy or SST) to several years of intensive work in psychoanalysis or a Jungian analysis. The length of your therapy will depend on the severity of the problems you brought to therapy, the goals you set, your expectations, and the theoretical orientation of the therapist. It is up to both the client and therapist to decide on the length of the therapy and what criteria are used to measure when you are ready to work on your own.

As we have seen, there is really no such thing as being "done" or "cured" in therapy. One measure may be that the original complaint has been resolved or the symptom eliminated. For example, your phobia of driving or of being at parties is no longer preventing you from doing the things you want to do.

Another way to understand when you are done with therapy is when you can think of yourself as being "on track" rather than as arriving at the end product of your initial goals. You have made some changes in behavior and have better ways to cope with life and its daily stressors. You feel you can handle what comes to you and know how to enlist the support of others.

104. Termination

Some therapists encourage the dependency we discussed above. After all, the client is a regular customer with a set hour or hours. She shows up on time, pays her bills, and isn't a problem for the therapist. To graduate this client is to give up a reliable stream of income. And after all, there is always more she can work on and talk about.

Therapy is about learning to use your own resources and abilities to live your life fully responsible for yourself. It's not about trading in the control and direction of your parents or spouse for the control and direction of a therapist, no matter how benevolent and wise your therapist seems to be. Therapy is about learning to be an adult and be on your own.

Termination is built into the concept of good therapy; capable, ethical therapists work with their clients to foster independence and freedom in their clients. They want them to develop confidence and assurance so that they can function without the therapist. They look for signs of this improvement so the client can graduate. They encourage their clients to see their own progress. Therapists who are not exploiting their clients financially encourage them to reduce the frequency of sessions when the clients are doing well and they encourage clients to work on their own.

In longer-term therapy, some therapists set a date of termination with a few months to wind up the major issues. In brief therapy, you begin therapy knowing you have only six or twelve sessions to accomplish your goals or get on track toward accomplishing them. In single session therapy (SST), you know you have one session to focus on what you want to accomplish. Then it's your job to do it, to follow through. The emphasis is on making changes quickly.

There is always the option to return if there is a temporary crisis, but being in therapy should not be the main part of your life.

You can think of it as an educational opportunity that you can continue on your own.

Therapy should not be interminable and go on for years and years. When it does, it may be an indication of the therapist's incompetence. If there is a constant focus on problems, the client can never be "done" because life will always bring problems and challenges to face. When a client is in therapy for years, the therapist may be exploiting the client economically because she can afford to continue indefinitely in therapy. It may also be a sign that the therapist and client have entered into a mutually dependent (or codependent) relationship that undermines the mental health of each. They are both "stuck."

When to terminate is best decided by therapist and client together with a clear understanding that the goals have been achieved, the client is on track, and has the tools he's learned in therapy to work on his own. If your therapist persists in putting off termination and says you're not ready, she may have her interests at heart more than yours. It may be up to you, the client, to exit so that you can become the independent person you want to be.

If you have been in therapy for more than fifty sessions with one therapist, take a session to evaluate your progress, your goals, and why you should or should not continue. You may want to rethink your goals or you may decide you want to work with someone else with a different focus. Endless therapies that go on for six, ten, fifteen, or twenty years suggest that the client is dependent on the therapist instead of becoming a more responsible adult. They may also suggest that the therapist is dependent on the client for continued economic support.

105. When to leave your therapist

In the practice of counseling and psychotherapy, there are some definite indicators to tell you to leave therapy with this therapist. Some of these have been suggested already, but deserve being listed below. Most of these are violations of the client/therapist boundaries. Some of these are unethical and/or illegal.

These include when your therapist:

a.   requests or initiates social contacts outside of the therapy hour

b.   asks for favors or advice from you

c.   intrudes into your personal life by expecting to be included in your family events or including you in his family gatherings

d.   shares personal problems with you or talks more about his interests and experiences than you do about yours

e.   expresses a personal attachment to you that is more than saying he likes you or values you in the context of therapy

f.   isolates you from others or consistently discourages other relationships

g.   falls asleep during your session or otherwise clearly demonstrates he is not paying attention

h.   takes phone calls frequently during your therapy hour and doesn't make up the time you've paid for

i.   uses sexist, racist, or ageist language or makes other comments that show prejudice, bigotry, or otherwise demonstrates a strong preference without acknowledging this bias

j.   calls you names or is otherwise verbally abusive, including yelling or shouting at you

k.   suggests physical or sexual contact with you

l.   refuses to discuss termination or your goals of therapy

m.   keeps you waiting past your appointed therapy hour without explanation or apology; is consistently late or behaves as if your time is not as valuable as his

n.   doesn't return your phone calls in a timely manner or doesn't return them at all

o.   uses the threat of hospitalization to control your behavior when you are not a danger to yourself or to others

p.   betrays a confidence by sharing your personal information with anyone else without your permission

q.   trivializes your concerns or is disrespectful of your feelings and beliefs by laughing at you or making fun of you

r.   refuses to answer your questions about treatment procedures and techniques

s.   tells you what is best for you without honoring your free dom of choice

t.   frequently keeps you beyond your scheduled time for more than a few minutes to "just talk"

In any of these situations, it is imperative for your own mental health for you to confront your therapist with your concerns. If the therapist does not respond to your satisfaction—perhaps with an apology and a change of behavior, then it's time to leave.

Most therapists are concerned and considerate of their clients, but there are those who are not. Some therapists have never resolved their own problems and so play them out in their therapy sessions with clients. If you find yourself in the hands of someone who does one or more of these unethical behaviors, leave. Do not be persuaded to continue your therapy unless you have discussed this with someone else you trust and who knows you. If you are unsure, ask another professional. Once again, you can call another therapist or ask to speak to someone who has some knowledge about what is proper behavior for this profession. You can call the licensing board and ask about the behavior in question.

Pay attention to your feelings. Ask questions!

And remember that if you have more psychological work to do, you can find a more ethical and competent therapist.

106. Changing therapists

Clients sometimes view changing therapists as a failure. "I can't even get along with my therapist," they might say. They may interpret their discomfort or disappointment with a therapist as an indication of their personal character defects.

In fact, many people who enter therapy decide at some point that the therapist is not the right one for them. This may or may not be because the therapist is doing something that is unethical or unacceptable to the client. As a potential client, you may simply feel that you aren't comfortable with a particular therapist, just as you might with any other professional. Perhaps you feel that you and the therapist don't share the same philosophy or "speak the same language."

Studies done on client/therapist communication reveal that this feeling is often based on measurable differences in communication styles. Perhaps you are speaking in more concrete, literal terminology and your therapist likes to tell stories or use metaphors and analogies. Or vice versa. Or perhaps one of you speaks quickly and doesn't finish sentences and the other

speaks slowly and in complex, complete, thoughtful para-
graphs. Other differences may include styles of expression and
gesture that might be culturally based, and the use of technical
or specialized jargon.

If English is not your first language, you might prefer to see a
therapist who can speak your native tongue so that you can
express yourself more fully and naturally. I believe that as much
as possible, clients should be able to speak in therapy to their
therapists the way they talk to themselves inside their own heads
and in the language they speak in their dreams and nightmares.
Usually, that will be the person's first spoken language.

Differences in personality can also account for the discomfort
a client may feel with a particular therapist. Ideally, a therapist
will match a client's pacing and style and create a comfortable
atmosphere, but sometimes the therapist is unable to do so.
Differences may be too great to bridge and it may be easier for
you to find a therapist with whom you feel rapport. Don't hesitate to do so. You can achieve more progress with a well-matched
therapist in one hour than you can in several sessions with someone who is a mismatch. Your comfort and sense of trust with
your therapist will make all the difference in your achieving your
goals and making the changes to have a more satisfying life. If
your difficulties with your therapist become the focus of your
therapy, you might simply do better with another therapist.

However, you may want to spend some time examining how
this desire to change therapists is part of your pattern of interacting with people in general. The problems you have in daily
living will surface in therapy and that is an excellent time to
examine them without the fear of negative consequences.

But if your interactions with your therapist just don't feel right and you can't open up, move on.

Remember that when choosing a therapist, don't hesitate to shop around and interview a few people over the phone to see if you are compatible. Sometimes taking a break from therapy and using some of the self-help techniques suggested later in this book can give you a better perspective on what course of action is best for you.

107. Trusting your own mind and feelings

Ultimately, the goal of all psychotherapy is to be more in touch with or aware of your own thoughts and feelings and to trust these as reliable sources of information. In therapy, you will learn that your decisions are best made by a combination of your rational mind and thoughts along with the balanced input of your feelings, sensations, and intuitions. Using only thoughts or feelings puts you at a disadvantage since neither can give you the whole picture alone. (LeDoux, Damasio) To grasp the levels of meaning in any situation, you need to have access to both rational thoughts and your emotions or gut reactions. To hear your "inner voice," you must listen with your mind and your body.

Therapy provides a practice ground for these skills, giving you tools to apply in new and unknown situations in the future. Over time, you will trust your ability to use these tools and will be able to trust your own mind and feelings.

This is your life and you are the final authority on who is the authentic you and on what is right for you.

108. Putting yourself in charge of your life

Ultimately, you are the one who is in charge of your life. Some time in therapy may have been spent on how you feel you have been a victim of your upbringing, the influence of your family, culture, and society. But in the final analysis, it is up to you to take charge of your life and your future. You are the one who must set your goals and chart your course for your future.

As a child, you didn't have either the choice or the skills to behave in ways that might have made your life different. But as a conscious, responsible adult, the choices are yours. You can make your life what you would like it to be and take the action necessary to accomplish what you want. You can see your obstacles realistically and overcome them with whatever power you have. You can know you are a product of your past experience and circumstances, but you don't have to let them define you or your future.

Even if you've felt like a victim in the past, you can choose not to be a victim in the future. You have learned from your mistakes and the mistakes of others. You are no longer blown about by the winds of chance and change; you have your own internal rudder. You determine your direction. You can listen to your inner voice and hear the many internal messages you send yourself. You can challenge them, change them, and question them. You hear your own music and you conduct your own orchestra. You are driving your own bus and you have the map.

While life may continue to offer you challenges and frustrations, you have the knowledge to know what you can act on and what you can't. You decide what meaning you give to any event. A successful therapy, whether it is one session or a thousand sessions, empowers you to act on the knowledge that you are in charge of your own life.

109. Lifelong learning

Throughout our lives, we have many problems thrown at us. Most of these do not require the assistance of a mental health professional. The earlier we learn the basic tools of coping, self-expression, managing our emotions, setting boundaries, and taking care of ourselves, the easier it is to deal with new problems as they arise. We also learn from our mistakes and disappointments.

Because there is no such thing as being done with personal growth and self-awareness, all of life is learning. Rather than expect to "get it together" or to "find yourself," as if these goals were finished products or endpoints, you can anticipate that life will always be a journey for learning new things. In many ways, being "on track" is this awareness of lifelong learning and an appreciation of the adventure.

110. Group therapy

Group formats for psychotherapy and personal growth provide some unique advantages over working alone with a therapist. Group members provide you with other points of view on a problem or the way you perceive something to be a problem. When they share their experiences, you are able to hear of other ways to respond to or interpret an event. You observe other ways of behaving and thinking that may serve as role models for you. Or they may serve as a "mirror" to show you how you appear to others when you behave or speak in similar ways. The group provides each member with feedback on how they are perceived by others in a setting that is usually more open and candid than ordinary gatherings of people. Hearing others with similar problems will also help you see you are not alone.

In individual psychotherapy, you, as the client, will hear only your therapist's point of view, suggestions, or interpretations in addition to your own. In group formats, there is a variety of perspectives that dilutes the power and impact of the therapist's words. This can diminish the possible pitfalls of becoming dependent on your therapist.

It may be difficult for someone to understand the impact their personality style has on others. Hearing it from just your therapist may not be enough to prompt you to consider alternative behaviors. But if you hear the same thing from six people in your group, you are more likely to seriously consider the merits of this criticism or point of view.

On the other hand, it is possible for groups to enter into a "groupthink" where certain assumptions aren't questioned and the group exercises peer pressure to get new members to conform to a particular way of thinking. This is especially dangerous, I believe, in homogeneous groups with members that have similar problems. After a while, they may all spout the same jargon and aphorisms. When members are hesitant to question these "truisms," the group goes stale. When pressure is strong to conform and admit rather than be accused of being in "denial," the client's autonomy may be threatened. Healthy groups allow you to express yourself and encourage disagreement and new ideas. There are no taboo topics or fear of dissension. (Goldhammer, Tart, Singer)

Be wary of groups that scapegoat individuals, have an ideology that you are expected to accept without question, or those that become insular or isolated from the rest of the environment or community.

As always, ask questions and speak your truth.

111. Alternatives to therapy: support groups

As more and more people have become psychologically aware of the need for psychological services, alternatives to psychotherapy have developed. These provide people with an opportunity to explore their histories, feelings, beliefs, and the way they behave or react to their life experiences. Support groups are usually free and gather people together who have similar issues. These concerns and the need for support might center on grief, coping with a family member with Alzheimer's or AIDS, parents of children with autism or specific learning disabilities, gay and lesbian groups, and people with a positive HIV status.

The groups are frequently offered by hospitals and health centers, often without fee. In these settings, the group leader may be a mental health professional or not. Sometimes people have good skills for group facilitation that encourage the group's development but who are not trained as psychologists or psychotherapists. These leaders may be paid by the facility or not. When they are paid, the facility provides the group as a public service as well as a way to let the public know about the treatment center and what other services are available for purchase. In merchandizing, this would be called a "loss leader," offering a product at below cost to get people in to buy other items at full price.

There is nothing wrong with this practice since they are offering a service that can be helpful to many people and some of those may need more help.

However, when the group becomes nothing more than a vehicle for selling the other services or pressing diagnoses of addiction onto the members for the purpose of drumming up business, then such a "support group" is really for the support of the facility. You will know if you have found such a group and can find another if you feel as if your presence is an opportunity to sell you products or services you don't think you need.

Local newspapers have lists of support groups with every imaginable focus. The newspapers usually run these announcements without charge as a public service, so you could start your own group in your area to meet your particular need. Meeting in a public, neutral space such as a restaurant or diner or library lobby will often bring out people who might be reluctant to go to a stranger's home. Be prepared to state what the group's goals and purpose are, but also know that these will evolve as the group changes in composition over time.

112. 12-Step groups

Beginning with Alcoholics Anonymous (AA), the recovery movement has provided a variety of 12-Step programs for people who want to work on themselves in a structured setting with others who acknowledge having similar problems. In addition to AA, there are now 12-Step programs available for drug addictions (Nar-Anon), codependency (CoDA), sexual addiction (SAA = Sex Addicts Anonymous), eating disorders (OA = Overeaters Anonymous or FAA = Fat Addicts Anonymous), shopping, gambling, and other problems, including groups that help those who have family members with a chemical dependency. These last groups include Adult Children of Alcoholics (ACOA) and Al-Anon for people who may be involved through work, family, or other relationship with someone who is an alcoholic or addict.

The groups usually follow a proscribed format of specific tasks and readings, usually ending with the Lord's Prayer. Originally based on a Christian concept of God, these groups have more recently acknowledged that your "higher power" is whatever you conceive it to be. You could say your higher power is within you, but most emphasis is placed on an external higher power of some kind. Individual groups re-word the Twelve Steps for their particular focus, especially in Step 1 that names the addiction's focus, but they are largely the same from group to group. In each case, the individual is expected to accept that he is "powerless" over the substance or behavior that is problematic and to turn their lives over to a Higher Power or God. In place of "God," some more secular groups have substituted "spiritual energy," or "God as we understand him" but this still implies a metaphysical force as change agent.

12-Step groups have offered insight and help to many, many people over the years who swear by their effectiveness and the positive difference the groups have made in their lives. Critics of 12-Step groups point out that the philosophy and format grew out of all male groups in another era of much less psychological understanding than we have today. The typical male pattern of alcoholism may include grandiosity, arrogance, aggression, violence, and a sense of entitlement. The humility and modesty required by the 12-Steps, including an examination of one's defects of character and an effort to make amends might be a viewpoint that was previously unknown to many of these men. Additionally, they may have been likely to become alcoholics to stifle the feelings that they were socialized to deny—even to themselves: fear, inadequacy, grief.

On the other hand, women have been socialized to be more aware of their feelings as well as to express them. They are taught to tune-in, be sensitive, and even be responsible for the feelings of others. (We now think of this latter behavior as codependent.) Many of the problems women experience come from finding fault with themselves when the problem may, in part, be their willingness to blame everything *on themselves*. In a patriarchal society, women have felt powerless, which has—for some—led to their sense of hopelessness and helplessness. These realties and perceptions (even when they are less than actual) are some of the main contributors to women's depression.

Author Charlotte Kasl and others, point out that perhaps a different format than the traditional 12-Steps would be more empowering for women and other marginalized groups such as ethnic, racial, and other minorities. The disease model of emotional or relationship problems and of substance abuse places the locus of control outside of you rather than within with the more helpful affirmation, "I can handle this." Unless you use the belief in an outside agency to mobilize your resources to overcome the outside force, then you are set up for more feelings of helplessness. You may come to see the group or the treatment system as the exclusive source of your recovery and depend on it for continued success and sobriety. You may believe, as 12-Step groups will tell you, that one drink or slip into the old behavior is the beginning of a crash toward a binge and a loss of all your achievements, which makes this outcome more likely if you backslide at all. You may not take credit for being able to monitor and measure your own behavior in your own way. This may rob you of feeling empowered and having a sense of self-agency: the very issues that may have made you vulnerable to addiction to begin with.

Stanton Peele, in *Diseasing of America,* discusses the research that says that most people recover from addiction on their own and without treatment. Giving up drug use is frequently part of the process of maturation and aging. Most people who used alcohol and drugs in their youth do not do so in middle age and most of them have not been to treatment. Indeed, smoking is one of the hardest addictions to overcome and ninety-five percent of all those who have quit smoking did it on their own without a program, group, or treatment system.

Recovery means getting on with your life as a fully functioning autonomous adult. It is of concern when the treatment (12-Step groups) becomes another way of life replacing bars and drug havens. If you are going to meetings instead of drinking and drugging, you might want to ask yourself what else has changed in your life that is evidence of you getting more mature, self-aware, and exercising your freedom as a unique individual.

113. Re-evaluation Counseling (RC), Co-counseling

Co-counseling, sometimes referred to as re-evaluation counseling is a system of therapeutic work based on the work of Harvey Jackins. Anyone can be trained to follow the basic steps of this model to help another. By working as peers and taking turns in the work, the system does not invite exploitation, dominance, or elitism.

The client comes to the counseling session with built up anger, fear, grief, and hurt from the experiences of her life, especially in childhood. By telling her story in her own way, the client can *discharge* these tensions and move forward. The counselor's function is to encourage the client to allow her feelings to surface and to stay with them through discharge, asking questions for clarification as needed. Clients and counselors both take full responsibility for themselves and their actions. While yelling and crying are encouraged, destruction of property is not acceptable discharge.

Because at the next session, the position of client and counselor are reversed, there are no fees paid. Outside the systems of conventional psychotherapy, the medical model, and insurance companies, the client and counselor don't have to deal with the red tape and intrusions of agencies. This model of counseling is used in many intentional communities.*

114. Self-therapy: art, writing, creative expression; personal journals/diaries

One of the most therapeutic avenues toward mental health and inner peace is finding a way to fully and safely express who you are at your deepest core. Through their artistic productions, sculptors, musicians, composers, painters, poets and writers have known the release that comes through the creative process.

---

* A directory of the hundreds of intentional communities around the world, including articles and information books on this subject, can be ordered at *http://www.ic.org*

Sometimes, making art is painful and stirs up old feelings and memories, but the translation of one's inner distress into an outward expression such as a dance, song, story, poem, or drawing, helps to bring closure and better understanding. You needn't think of yourself as creative or talented to use these methods to express emotions. Doodling is something you probably did in school and still do at meetings. This is your natural inclination to find an outlet for your feelings and thoughts. The idea is not to create Art, though that might develop if you decide to master the craft of any of these forms. What you are doing by writing, drawing, or using movement, is getting the troubling feelings or thoughts out into the world in a way that you can see them, and in a way that doesn't hurt others. If you are feeling angry, your anger is likely to leak out and hurt those whom you love the most. If you write about your anger, much of it will dissipate and you may have a different perspective or a different grasp of what you were angry about before you started writing about it. Making it into a fictional story gives you the opportunity to rewrite lousy endings or to get even in the story when it's impossible or unwise to get even in your life.

For all of my psychotherapy clients who show an interest, I recommend keeping a personal journal. At first, most balk at the time and effort it takes, but those who have written in a journal every day for a few weeks, begin to value this process. Some of the stuck feelings and the heaviness they brought to therapy lift; much of their anxiety diminishes after writing a few pages, no matter how jumbled the content. (Cameron, Adams, Rainer)

Studies on people who write about their darkest secrets and pain show that while they initially feel worse, they show improved functioning and mood in the long run. Such disclosure, when it is deep and heartfelt, also boosts the functioning of the immune system.

Write every day, preferably at the same time every day, and preferably in the morning when you first get up and are closest to your unconscious. This the time to record whatever comes to mind without censoring the way you say it or being polite, proper, or politically correct. This is the place where you can have your say, can piss and moan, gripe and bitch, curse and complain. You can sound infantile and whiny; you can be a bastard. And you don't have to watch your language.

No one sees this journal. It is not necessary that you re-read what you write though it can be helpful when it is read from some distance in time. The process of writing, of ventilating, of hearing yourself say the same things over and over again is what is helpful, just as these aspects of psychotherapy have beneficial and healing value. Doing this on your own, you will come to know yourself in a way you might not otherwise.

After some time of keeping the journal steadily, you will notice patterns in your speech, your thinking, and the things that distress you. Reading back, you will also see how often you obsessed and worried over things that seem trivial or comical now. You worried over things that never happened. The worst things turned out to be blessings in disguise. (And don't you hate it when people tell you that in the middle of your distress?) This helps you to face life's turmoil with more peace of mind in the future. You truly know that this, too, shall pass. And you learn what your resources are. The next time adversity hits, you can say, "I've handled worse than this before. I'll make it this time, too." The journal helps to remind you of these strengths.

We have a tendency to remember our failures instead of our successes. By keeping a journal, we record both and can see all of what we label success or failure has elements of the other. Each experience is a part of our lifelong learning. A journal is a personal account of our private education.

115. Forming your own network of support and encouragement

As you move toward confidence and self-acceptance, you will want to continue to be connected to others who support your growth. People who best support you are those who are not only willing to encourage you and remind you of your strengths, but those who will also question and challenge you. These are the friends who will lovingly confront you when you are being less than honest or when you are backsliding into the patterns you wanted to change. These are the people who will set boundaries for themselves even when they apply to you.

When choosing friends to be part of your network of support and encouragement, choose those who have the traits you want to emulate. If you are shy and would like to feel more comfortable when interacting with others or in new situations, choose to be with people who have this confidence and social skills you can observe. You might even ask them to invite you to do things that you know are hard for you but you'd like to do.

If you want to be a writer, join a group of writers or cultivate a friendship with one. Seek out people who have achieved the goals you aspire toward. Ask them what they do and how they overcome their own blocks to accomplish what they want. People love to talk about themselves and brag about their successes. You can learn by listening and observing and experimenting with new behavior.

Be wary of people who find fault with your creative ideas or discourage you to take risks. If they say, "That won't work," ask them why. If someone is being negative, I want them to give me evidence for their point of view or I just write them off as negative people. Constructive criticism can be helpful—especially if someone has knowledge and experience I don't and can share it with me. But if they are just looking at the dark side then I wonder if they are discouraging my possible success out of jealousy or their own insecurity. Such people can be toxic for your future growth. Disconnect as soon as you can or limit your time and exposure to such people if you must see them because they are family or co-workers. Develop a "take it from whence it comes" mentality. Don't let them drag you down to their level of mediocrity or worse. (Cameron)

In addition, be careful to choose your support people from those who have demonstrated good coping skills, strength of character, and the principles and ethical vision that are compatible with your own. Choose from people who are ahead of where you think you are emotionally and intellectually. Let them challenge you and provide you with an example of living with higher standards and bigger goals than what you've been surrounded by so far. Ask them directly to bolster your growth and self-improvement. Tell them when you need their praise and validation.

116. Advocates, mentors, and teachers

Part of your support system may be people who are mentors, teachers, or advocates. Many of us are fortunate enough to meet people in the course of our lives who show an interest in us and who offer guidance and teaching without being asked. Sometimes this happens in a formal setting in school, but many times it happens informally when someone—a neighbor, a distant relative, a friend's parent—recognizes our potential and helps to provide encouragement or coaching so that we can grow.

Those people who have had painful and difficult childhoods but come out successful and triumphant over their personal tragedies have often had others in their lives who stepped in and provided the support that was missing from their families. As important as having these people in their lives, they had the wisdom to allow these benefactors to mentor them. They accepted the guidance and allowed their self-image to be transformed. They permitted others to believe in them when they didn't believe in themselves—until they did believe in themselves. It may have been only one teacher in elementary school that encouraged the child to overcome a fear of learning. It may have been a clergy person who discovered a talent or simply said, "I know you can do what you want to do. I believe in you."

Such moments can provide the difference between a lifetime of despair and a lifetime of realized dreams. What is even more hopeful is that you can be on the lookout for people who can provide you with this kind of mentoring and support. When you let others know you want to learn, are willing to accept coaching or tutoring, people will appear to help you. One of the great pleasures in life is to share the wealth of our knowledge and skill with others and see them experience the joy of learning and stretching themselves to be all they can be.

In your own life, think about people you admire. Think about people you emulate or see as a role model. Who are they? How can they be of help to you? What would you like to ask them? What information might they have to share with you about their success or their satisfaction in life? Would they be willing to give you advice or guidance?

Ask. You never know what door you might open for yourself by being willing to have another person act as a temporary guide.

Another way to enlist the support of someone you admire is to volunteer for them. If they give seminars you would like to attend but can't afford, offer to go as an assistant instead of paying the fee. Many organizations are happy to allow people to work for a day or more to handle registrations or product sales or some other task in exchange for admission to the workshop. A single day can provide the bridge to begin making the larger changes you want to make in your life.

Notice that I am not suggesting that your therapist be this person for whom you volunteer. This holds all the risks of having a dual relationship (client plus employee or volunteer) and may increase your dependency on your therapeutic relationship. I am suggesting you seek out *other* people in the fields you want to explore (writing, art, small business, speaking, fitness, health) to be exposed to people who will either be role models for you or mentor you more closely.

If you are reading this book because you have had a long history of negative experiences with mental health professionals, you might consider finding an advocate. Many organizations offer support and information to those abused by psychiatry and psychology. Many of these can be found on the World Wide Web or listed in Paula Caplan's book, *They Say You're Crazy.*

117. Body work for self-awareness and stability: yoga, meditation, music, dance, massage, exercise

Body work, whether you do it or someone does it to you (massage) is another way to release pent up emotions and tensions. You may want to take up an exercise program that appeals to you. Try several and see what you like. Just walking can restore your emotional balance when you are feeling strung-out, stressed, or angry. Get a professional massage or exchange a massage with a friend to keep the cost down. Inquire at your local community center or gym about the classes offered. A regular yoga class works for me. Discover what works for you.

Meditation is another avenue instead of psychotherapy to gain inner knowledge and peace. Basic classes are offered in community schools, centers, and at ashrams. You can also learn the basic techniques of meditation from a book. (Kornfield, Goldstein, Hanh, LeShan, Tart)

118. Workshops and personal growth seminars

There are many large group seminars in personal growth, usually offered for a weekend or a few days. These can be educational and helpful. Many of them have received a lot of publicity in the last twenty years regarding their effectiveness and their dangers. If you decide to take a weekend workshop, remember that a group setting has built-in factors that increase your suggestibility. Many of these workshops are the start of more and more courses at ever-increasing cost, promising transformation without explaining exactly what that means. They may also ask you to volunteer your time to promote the workshops, enlist other attendees, and spend more time with others associated with the particular workshop type. While you may learn a lot, you may also be slowly giving up your own goals and autonomy in favor of those set by group leaders. Excessive volunteer work will eat up your time and energy to pursue your personal goals and relationships. If you find yourself increasingly involved with any one group or activity, you might question the longer term benefits. (Singer) If you take a basic weekend in one of these formats, give yourself some time and distance to assimilate and review what you learned before jumping into more classes and courses.

119. Bibliotherapy: self-help books and tapes, reading for mental and emotional health

Another way to improve your mental health and self-awareness instead of therapy is to study self-help books and tapes. The extensive bibliography at the end of this book includes many authors whose work has proved helpful to people who could not afford formal psychotherapy or chose not to enter therapy. In particular, Stephen R. Covey and Martin Seligman write books in plain language that can get you on track to feeling better and living a more satisfying life. Explore the many self-help audio tapes that address the problems that concern you and see what you can do for yourself. Listening to educational tapes in the car is one way to productively use the time when you travel or are stuck in traffic.

120. Taking personal growth and self-awareness into action; Making changes in your life

Therapy or any path of personal growth can bring insight into who we are. It may point to the causes of our behavior and how we got to be who we are. Sometimes we learn the original reason we adapted a pattern of reaction and response. We might say that we know we are fearful because we have been wounded as children by people whom we should have been able to rely on for nurturing and support. Or perhaps we had a traumatic event along the way that left us cautious or less likely to be trusting of others.

Knowing causes and origins is only part of resolving our mental and emotional distress. To get better and be all we can be, we must take our insights into action. It is up to each of us to make changes in our lives, whether based upon our own defects of character or caused by others who have hurt us. As adults, it is up to us to use what we learn to improve and grow and to help others to do the same.

Be cautious and wise in your plan for self-improvement, whether through therapy or self-therapy.

And remember to ask questions.

Bibliography

Adams, Kathleen. *Journal to the Self: Twenty-Two Paths to Personal Growth*. Warner 1990.

Adler, Margot. *Drawing Down the Moon*. Penguin/Arkana. 1986.

Aftel, Mandy, & Lakoff, Robin Tolmach. *When Talk is Not Cheap: How to Find the Right Therapist When You Don't Know Where to Begin*. Warner. 1985

Alvarez, A. *Night: Night Life, Night Language, Sleep, and Dreams*. W.W. Norton. 1995.

Amada, Gerald. *A Guide to Psychotherapy*. Ballantine. 1983.

Anand, Margo. *The Art Of Sexual Ecstasy: The Path of Sacred Sexuality for Western Lovers*. Jeremy P. Tarcher. 1989.

Anapol, Deborah M. *Love Without Limits*. IntiNet. 1992

Andreas, Connirae, & Andreas, T. *Core Transformation: Reaching the Wellspring Within*. Real People Press. 1994.

Andreas, Steve, & Andreas, Connirae. *Heart of the Mind: Engaging Your Inner Power to Change with Neuro-Linguistic Programming*. Real People Press. 1987.

Andreas, Steve, & Andreas, Connirae. *Change Your Mind—and Keep the Change*. Real People Press. 1987.

Antony, Martin M. & Swinson, Richard. *When Perfect Isn't Good Enough: Strategies For Coping with Perfectionism.* New Harbinger. 1998.

Armstrong, Thomas. *7 Kinds of Smart: Identifying and Developing Your Multiple Intelligences.* Plume. 1993.

Aron, Elaine N. *The Highly Sensitive Person: How to Thrive When the World Overwhelms You.* Broadway. 1996.

Assagioli, Roberto. *Psychosynthesis: A Manual of Principles and Techniques.* Viking Press. 1965.

Assagioli, Roberto. *The Act of Will.* Penguin. 1973.

Baker, Robert A. *Mind Games: Are We Obsessed with Therapy?* Prometheus. 1996.

Baker, Robert A. *Hidden Memories: Voices and Visions from Within.* Prometheus. 1992.

Bandler, Richard. and Macdonald, W. *An Insider's Guide to Sub-Modalities.* Meta Publications. 1988.

Bandler, Richard, and Grinder, John. *Reframing.* Real People Press. 1982.

Bandler, Richard, and Grinder, John. *Time for a Change.* Meta Publications. 1993.

Bandler, Richard, and Grinder, John. *Frogs into Princes.* Real People Press. 1979.

Bandler, Richard, and Grinder, John. *Using Your Brain...For a Change.* Real People Press. 1985.

Bandler, Richard, and Grinder, John. *Trance-Formations*. Real People Press. 1981

Barbach, Lonnie Garfield. *For Yourself: The Fulfillment of Female Sexuality*. Anchor. 1976.

Barker, Dan. *Maybe Yes, Maybe No: A Guide for Young Skeptics*. Prometheus. 1990.

Barker, Philip. *Using Metaphors in Psychotherapy*. Brunner/Mazel. 1985

Bass, Ellen, and Davis, L. *The Courage to Heal*. HarperPerennial. 1988.

Bateson, Gregory. *Steps to an Ecology of Mind: A Revolutionary Approach to Man's Understanding Himself*. Ballantine. 1972.

Beattie, Melody. *Codependent No More*. Harper/Hazelden. 1987.

Beattie, Melody. *Beyond Codependency*. Harper/Hazelden. 1989.

Beck, Judith S. *Cognitive Therapy*. Guilford Press. 1995.

Bergman, Ronald. *Emotional Fitness Conditioning*. Perigee. 1998

Bersoff, Donald N. *Ethical Issues in Psychology*. American Psychological Association. 1995.

Beutler, Larry, and Bongar, Shurkin. *Am I Crazy, or is It My Shrink? How to Get the Help You Need*. Oxford University Press. 1998.

Bilodeau, Lorrainne. *The Anger Workbook*. Hazelden. 1992.

Blanton, Brad. *Radical Honesty*. Dell. 1994.

Blatner, Adam. *Acting In: Practical Applications Of Psychodramatic Methods*. Springer Publishing Company. 1988

Bly, Robert. *A Little Book on the Human Shadow*. HarperSanFrancisco. 1988.

Boldt, Laurence G. *Zen and the Art of Making a Living*. Penguin/Arkana. 1992.

Boldt, Laurence G. *How to Find the Work You Love*. Penguin/Arkana. 1996.

Bolles, Richard N. *The Three Boxes of Life and How to Get Out of Them*. Ten Speed Press. 1981.

Bolles, Richard N. *What Color is Your Parachute?* Ten Speed Press. 1997.

Borcherdt, Bill. *Think Straight! Feel Great!* Professional Resource Exchange, Inc. 1989.

Borcherdt, Bill. *You Can Control Your Feelings! 24 Guides to Emotional Well-Being*. Professional Resource Press. 1993.

Bradshaw, John. *Family Secrets: The Path to Self-Acceptance and Reunion*. Bantam. 1995.

Bradshaw, John. *Healing the Shame that Binds You*. Health Communications. 1988.

Braham, Barbara J. *Finding Your Purpose*. Crisp. 1991.

Bramson, Robert M. *Coping with Difficult People*. Dell. 1991.

Branden, Nathaniel. *Six Pillars of Self-Esteem*. Bantam. 1994.

Breggin, Peter. *Electro-Shock: Its Brain-Disabling Effects.* Springer. 1979.

Breggin, Peter, and Breggin, Ginger Ross. *Talking Back To Prozac.* St. Martin's Press. 1994

Breggin, Peter. *Beyond Conflict.* St. Martin's Press. 1992.

Breggin, Peter R. *Toxic Psychiatry.* St. Martin's Press. 1991.

Buchholz, Ester Schaler. *The Call of Solitude: Alonetime in a World of Attachment.* Simon & Schuster. 1997.

Butler, Gillian, and Hope, Tony. *Managing Your Mind: The Mental Fitness Guide.* Oxford University Press. 1995.

Cameron, Julia. *The Artist's Way: A Spiritual Path to Higher Creativity.* Jeremy P. Tarcher/Putnam. 1992.

Cameron, Julia. *The Vein Of Gold: A Journey to Your Creative Heart.* Jeremy P. Tarcher/Putnam. 1996.

Capacchione, Lucia. *The Creative Journal: The Art of Finding Yourself.* Newcastle. 1979.

Capaldi, Nicholas. *The Art of Deception: An Introduction to Critical Thinking.* Prometheus. 1987.

Caplan, Paula J. *The Myth of Women's Masochism.* E.P. Dutton. 1985.

Caplan, Paula J. *They Say You're Crazy: The Inside Story of the DSM.* Addison-Wesley Publishing. 1995.

Carlson, Richard, and Shield, Benjamin, editors. *Healers on Healing.* Jeremy P. Tarcher. 1989.

Carlson, Richard. *Don't Sweat the Small Stuff.* Hyperion. 1997.

Carnes, Patrick. *Out of the Shadows: Understanding Sexual Addiction.* Hazelden. 1992.

Chandler, Steve. *100 Ways to Motivate Yourself.* Career Press. 1996.

Chavkin, Samuel. *The Mind Stealers: Psychosurgery and Mind Control.* Houghton Mifflin. 1978.

Cialdini, Robert B. *Influence: The Psychology of Persuasion.* Quill/William Morrow. 1993.

Cleveland, Martha, and Arlys G. *The Alternative 12 Steps: A Secular Guide to Recovery.* Health Communications. 1992.

Conway, Flo, and Siegelman, Jim. *Snapping: America's Epidemic of Sudden Personality Change.* Stillpoint Press. 1978.

Covey, Stephen R. *The 7 Habits of Highly Effective People.* Simon & Schuster. 1989.

Covey, Stephen R., Merill, A. Roger, and Merrill, Rebecca R. *First Things First.* Simon & Schuster. 1995.

Covey, Stephen R., Merill, A. Roger, and Merrill, Rebecca R. *Daily Reflections for Highly Effective People.* Simon & Schuster. 1994.

Crisp, Wendy Reid. *100 Things I'm Not Going to Do Now That I'm 50.* Perigee. 1995.

Csikszentmihalyi, Mihali. *Creativity: Flow and the Psychology of Discovery and Invention.* HarperCollins. 1996.

Csikszentmihalyi, Mihali. *Flow: The Psychology of Optimal Experience*. HarperPerrenial. 1990.

Csikszentmihalyi, Mihali. *The Evolving Self*. HarperPerrenial. 1993

Damasio, Antonio. *The Feeling of What Happens: Body and Emotion in the Making of Consciousness*. Harcourt Brace & Company. 1999.

Damasio, Antonio. *Descartes' Error*. Avon. 1994

Dayton, Tian. *Drama Games: Techniques for Self-Development*. Health Communications. 1990.

Dayton, Tian. *The Drama Within: Psychodrama and Experiential Therapy*. Health Communications. 1994.

De Becker, Gavin. *The Gift Of Fear: Survival Signals that Protect Us from Violence*. Little, Brown, and Company. 1997.

De Bono, Edward. *Six Thinking Hats*, Little, Brown and Company. 1985.

De Bono, Edward. *Practical Thinking*. Penguin. 1971.

De Bono, Edward. *Lateral Thinking: Creativity Step By Step*. Harper and Row. 1970.

De Bono, Edward. *De Bono's Thinking Course*. Fact on File. 1982.

De Shazer, Steve. *Clues: Investigating Solutions in Brief Therapy*. W.W. Norton. 1988.

De Shazer, Steve. *Words Were Originally Magic*. W.W. Norton. 1995.

Deacon, Terrence W. *The Symbolic Species: The Co-Evolution of Language and the Brain*. W.W. Norton. 1997.

Deikman, Arthur J. *The Observing Self: Mysticism and Psychotherapy*. Beacon Press. 1982.

Deikman, Arthur J. *The Wrong Way Home: Uncovering the Patterns of Cult Behavior in American Society*. Beacon Press. 1994.

Delaney, Gayle. *Breakthrough Dreaming: How to Tap the Power of Your 24-Hour Mind*. Bantam. 1991.

Dennett, Daniel C. *Kinds of Minds: Toward an Understanding of Consciousness*. BasicBooks. 1996.

Dershowitz, Alan M. *The Abuse Excuse*. Little, Brown and Company. 1994.

Dilts, Robert. *Changing Belief Systems with NLP*. Meta Publications. 1990.

Dolan, Yvonne M. *Resolving Sexual Abuse: Solution-Focused Therapy and Ericksonian Hypnosis for Adult Survivors*. W.W. Norton. 1991.

Dominguez, Joe, and Robin, Vicki. *Your Money or Your Life*. Penguin. 1992.

Dryden, Windy, and DiGiuseppe, Raymond. *A Primer on Rational-Emotive Therapy*. Research Press. 1990.

Eberle, Paul and Eberle, Shirley. *The Abuse of Innocence: The McMartin Preschool Trial*. Prometheus. 1993.

Ehrenberg, Otto, and Ehrenberg, Miriam. *The Psychotherapy Maze: A Consumer's Guide to Getting in and Out of Therapy*. Jason Aronson, Inc. 1986.

Elgin, Suzette Haden. *How To Disagree Without Being Disagreeable*. John Wiley & Sons. 1997.

Ellis, Albert, and Yeager, Raymond J. *Why Some Therapies Don't Work: The Dangers of Transpersonal Psychology*. Prometheus. 1989.

Ellis, Albert, and Harper, Robert A. *A New Guide to Rational Living*. Wilshire Book Company. 1961.

Etzioni, Amitai. *The Spirit of Community: The Reinvention of American Society*. Touchstone, Simon & Schuster. 1993.

Faraday, Ann. *Dream Power*. Berkley Medallion. 1972.

Faraday, Ann. *The Dream Game*. Perennial/Harper & Row. 1974.

Ferrucci, Piero. *What We May Be: Techniques for Psychological and Spiritual Growth through Psychosynthesis*. Jeremy P. Tarcher. 1982.

Fisch, Richard; Weakland, John, and Segal, Lynn. *The Tactics of Change: Doing Therapy Briefly*. Jossey-Bass. 1982.

Fisher, Roger, and Ury, William. *Getting to Yes: Negotiating Agreement without Giving In*. Penguin. 1981.

Forward, Susan, with Donna Frazier. *Emotional Blackmail*. HarperCollins. 1997.

Forward, Susan, with Craig Buck. *Toxic Parents: Overcoming Their Hurtful Legacy and Reclaiming Your Life*. Bantam. 1989.

Foster, Steven, with Meredith Little. *The Book of the Vision Quest*. Simon & Schuster. 1992.

Fox, John. Poetic Medicine: *The Healing Art of Poem-Making.* Jeremy P. Tarcher/Putnam. 1997.

Fox, John. *Finding What You Didn't Lose: Expressing Your Truth and Creativity Through Poem-Making.* Jeremy P. Tarcher. 1995.

Jonathan, *The Essential Moreno.* Springer Publishing. 1987.

Freud, Sigmund. *Delusion and Dream.* Beacon Press. 1956.

Freud, Sigmund. *Therapy and Technique.* Crowell/Collier. 1963.

Freud, Sigmund. *Psychopathology of Everyday Life.* Mentor/Macmillon. 1951.

Freud, Sigmund. *Three Contributions to the Theory of Sex.* Dutton. 1962.

Freud, Sigmund. *Group Psychology and the Analysis of the Ego.* W.W. Norton. 1959.

Friedberg, John. *The Mind Stealers: Shock Treatment Is Not Good for Your Brain.* Glide Publications. 1976.

Fritz, Robert. *The Path of Least Resistance: Learning to Become a Creative Force in Your Own Life.* Fawcett Columbine. 1989.

Fritz, Roger. *Sleep Disorders: America's Hidden Nightmare.* National Sleep Alert, Inc. 1993.

Fromm, Erich. *Psychoanalysis and Religion.* Yale University Press. 1950.

Fross, Garland H. *Handbook of Hypnotic Techniques.* Florida Hypnosis Center. 1988.

Gabor, Don. *Speaking Your Mind in 101 Difficult Situations.* Fireside/Simon & Schuster. 1994.

Galanter, Marc. *Cults: Faith, Healing, and Coercion.* Oxford University Press. 1989.

Gallegos, Eligio Stephen. *The Personal Totem Pole: Amimal Imagery, The Chakras, and Psychotherapy.* Moon Bear Press. 1985.

Gardner, Howard. *Multiple Intelligences: The Theory in Practice, a Reader.* BasicBooks. 1993.

Gardner, Howard. *Frames of Mind: The Theory of Multiple Intelligences.* BasicBooks. 1983.

Gardner, Howard. *Extraordinary Minds.* BasicBooks. 1997.

Gelb, Michael J. *How to Think Like Leonardo Da Vinci: Seven Steps to Genius Every Day.* Delacorte. 1998.

Gendlin, Eugene T. *Focusing.* Bantam. 1978.

Gendlin, Eugene T. *Let Your Body Interpret Your Dreams.* Chiron Publications. 1986.

Glass, Lillian. *Toxic People: 10 Ways of Dealing with People Who Make Your Life Miserable.* St. Martin's Griffin. 1995.

Glasser, William. *Positive Addiction.* Harper & Row. 1976.

Goldberg, Natalie. *Long Quiet Highway.* Bantam. 1993.

Goldberg, Natalie. *Wild Mind: Living the Writer's Life.* Bantam. 1990.

Goldberg, Natalie. *Writing Down the Bones: Freeing the Writer Within*. Shambhala. 1986.

Goldhammer, John D. *Under the Influence: The Destructive Effects of Group Dynamics*. Prometheus. 1996.

Goldstein, Joseph, and Kornfield, Jack. *Seeking the Heart of Wisdom: The Path of Insight Meditation*. Shambhala. 1987.

Goldstein, Joseph. *The Experience of Insight: A Simple and Direct Guide to Buddhist Meditation*. Shambhala. 1976.

Goleman, Daniel. *Emotional Intelligence*. Bantam Books. 1995.

Goleman, Daniel. *Vital Lies, Simple Truths: The Psychology of Self-Deception*. Touchstone/Simon & Schuster. 1985.

Gottman, John, with Nan Silver. *Why Marriages Succeed or Fail*. Simon & Schuster. 1994.

Gottman, John, with Nan Silver. *The Seven Prinicples for Making Marriage Work*. Crown/Random House. 1999.

Gough, Russell W. *Character is Destiny: The Value of Personal Ethics in Everyday Life*. Forum/Prima Publishing. 1998.

Green, Tova, and Woodrow, Peter, with Fran Peavey. *Insight and Action*. New Society. 1994.

Griffith, & Levinson, D. & Levinson, M. *Complete Guide to Psychotherapy Drugs and Psychological Disorders*. Perigee. 1997.

Grof, Stanislav, and Grof, Christina, editors. *Spiritual Emergency: When Personal Transformation Becomes A Crisis*. Jeremy P. Tarcher. 1989.

Hadley, Josie, and Staudacher, Carol. *Hypnosis for Change: A Practical Manual of Proven Hypnotic Techniques.* New Harbinger. 1989.

Haley, Jay. *Problem-Solving Therapy, 2nd ed.* Jossey-Bass. 1987.

Hammerschlag, Carl A. and Silverman, Howard. *Healing Ceremonies.* Perigee. 1997.

Hanh, Thich Nhat. *The Miracle of Mindfulness: A Manual on Meditation.* Beacon Press. 1975.

Hare, Robert D. *Without Conscience: The Disturbing World of the Psychopaths Among Us.* Pocket. 1993.

Hassan, Steven. *Combatting Cult Mind Control.* Park Street Press. 1988.

Havens, Leston. A SAFE PLACE. Ballantine. 1989.

Hendricks, Gay & Kathlyn. *Conscious Loving: The Journey to Co-Commitment.* Bantam. 1990.

Hendricks, Gay & Kathlyn. *The Conscious Heart: Seven Soul-Choices that Create Your Relationship Destiny.* Bantam. 1997.

Hendricks, Gay. *Conscious Breathing: Breathwork for Health, Stress Release, and Personal Mastery.* Bantam. 1995

Hendrix, Harville, and Hunt, Helen. *The Couples Companion: Meditations and Exercises for Getting the Love You Want.* Pocket. 1994.

Hendrix, Harville. *Getting the Love You Want: A Guide for Couples.* HarperPerennial. 1988.

Hendrix, Harville. *Keeping the Love You Find: A Guide for Singles.* Pocket. 1992.

Hendrix, Harville, and Hunt, Helen. *The Personal Companion: Meditations and Exercises for Keeping the Love You Find.* Pocket. 1995.

Hendrix, Harville, and Hunt, Helen. *Giving the Love that Heals.* Pocket. 1997.

Hewitt, William H. *Hypnosis: A Power Program for Self-Improvement, Changing Your Life, and Helping Others.* Llewellyn. 1986.

Hillman, James. *The Soul's Code: In Search of Character and Calling.* Random House. 1996.

Hillman, James, and Ventura, Michael. *We've Had a Hundred Years of Psychotherapy and the World's Getting Worse.* HarperSanFransciso. 1992.

Hillman, James, *A Blue Fire.* HarperPerennial. 1989.

Hoffer, Eric. *The True Believer.* Perennial. 1951.

Horn, Sam. *Tongue Fu! How to Deflect, Disarm, and Defuse Any Verbal Conflict.* St. Martin's Griffin. 1996.

Horney, Karen. *New Ways in Psychoanalysis.* W.W. Norton. 1939.

Horney, Karen. *Are You Considering Psychoanalysis?* W.W. Norton. 1946.

Horney, Karen. *Neurosis and Human Growth.* W.W. Norton. 1950.

Horney, Karen. *The Neurotic Personality of Our Time*. W.W. Norton. 1937.

Horney, Karen. *Feminine Psychology*. W.W. Norton. 1967.

Horney, Karen. *Self-Analysis*. W.W. Norton. 1942.

Houston, Jean. THE POSSIBLE HUMAN: *A Course in Enhancing Your Physical, Mental, and Creative Abilities*. Jeremy P. Tarcher. 1982.

Hoyt, Michael F. *Brief Therapy and Managed Care: Readings for Contemporary Practice*. Jossey-Bass. 1995.

Hoyt, Michael F. *Constructive Therapies. Vol. 1*. Guilford Press. 1994

Hoyt, Michael F. *Constructive Therapies. Vol. 2*. Guilford Press. 1996.

Huber, Cheri. *Being Present in the Darkness: Depression as an Opportunity for Self-Discovery*. Perigee. 1991.

Huber, Cheri. *Be the Person You Want to Find*. Keep It Simple Books. 1997.

Huber, Cheri. *There is Nothing Wrong with You*. Keep It Simple Books. 1993.

Hughes, Robert. *Culture of Complaint: A Passionate Look into the Ailing Heart of America*. Warner. 1972.

Jack, Dana Crowley. *Silencing the Self: Women and Depression*. HarperPerrenial. 1991.

Jackins. Harvey. *Fundamentals of Co-Counseling Manual*. Rational Island Publishers. 1982.

Janov, Arthur. *The Primal Scream—Primal Therapy: The Cure for Neurosis*. Dell. 1970.

Johnson, Robert A. *Owning Your Own Shadow: Understanding the Dark Side of the Psyche*. HarperSanFrancisco. 1991.

Johnson, Robert A. *Inner Work: Using Dreams & Active Imagination for Personal Growth*. HarperSanFrancisco. 1986.

Johnson, Catherine. *When to Say Goodbye to Your Therapist*. Simon & Schuster. 1988.

Jourard, Sidney M. *The Transparent Self*. Van Nostrand. 1971.

Jung, C.G. *Memories, Dreams, and Reflections*. Vintage. 1989.

Jung, Carl G. *Man and His Symbols*. Dell. 1964.

Kabat-Zinn, Jon. *Wherever You Go, There You Are: Mindfulness Meditation in Everyday Life*. Hyperion. 1994.

Kaminer, Wendy. *I'm Dysfunctional, You're Dysfunctional: The Recovery Movement and Other Self-Help Fashions*. Vintage. 1993.

Kasl, Charlotte Davis. *Women, Sex, And Addiction: A Search for Love and Power*. Harper & Row. 1989.

Kasl, Charlotte Davis. *Many Roads, One Journey: Moving Beyond the 12 Steps*. HarperPerennial. 1992.

Kegan, Robert. *In Over Our Heads: The Mental Demands of Modern Life*. Harvard University Press. 1994.

Kegan, Robert. *The Evolving Self: Problem and Process in Human Development*. Harvard University Press. 1982.

Keyes, Ken. *The Power of Unconditional Love: 21 Guidelines For beginning, Improving, and Changing Your Most Meaningful Relationships.* Love Line Books. 1990.

Kidder, Rushworth M. *How Good People Make Tough Choices.* Fireside/Simon & Schuster. 1995.

Kingma, Daphne Rose. *Coming Apart.* MJF Books. 1987.

Knott, Leonard L. *Writing for the Joy of It.* Writers Digest. 1983.

Kornfield, Jack. *A Path with Heart: A Guide Through the Perils And Promises Of Spiritual Life.* Bantam. 1993.

Krakow, Barry Joseph Neidhardt. *Conquering Bad Dreams & Nightmares: A Guide to Understanding, Interpretation, And Cure.* Berkley. 1992.

Kramer, Peter D. *Should You Leave?* Scribner. 1997.

Kramer, Peter D. *Listening to Prozac.* Viking. 1993.

Kramer, Peter D. *Moments of Engagement: Intimate Psychotherapy in a Technological Age.* Penguin. 1989

Kratz, Dennis M., Kratz, Abby Robinson. *Effective Listening Skills.* Career Press. 1993.

Kryger, Meir, Roth, and Dement, W. *Principles and Practice of Sleep Medicine.* W.B. Saunders Company. 1994.

Kuhn, Cynthia, and Swartzwelder, Scott, and Wilson, Wilkie. *Buzzed: Most Used and Abused Drugs.* W.W. Norton. 1998.

Kurtz, Paul. *Exuberance: An Affirmative Philosophy of Life.* Prometheus Books. 1985.

LaBerge, Stephen. *Lucid Dreaming: The Power of Being Awake and Aware in Your Dreams.* Ballantine Books. 1985.

Laborde, Genie Z. *Influencing with Integrity.* Syntony Publishing. 1997.

Lakein, Alan. *How to Get Control of Your Time and Your Life.* Signet. 1973.

Langone, Michael D. (ed.) *Recovery from Cults: Help for Victims of Psychological and Spiritual Abuse.* W.W. Norton. 1993.

LeDoux, Joseph. *The Emotional Brain: The Mysterious Underpinnings of Emotional Life.* Touchstone/Simon & Schuster. 1996.

Lee, John, with Bill Stott. *Facing the Fire: Experiencing and Expressing Anger Appropriately.* Bantam. 1993.

Lerner, Harriet. *The Dance of Intimacy.* HarperPerrenial. 1989.

Lerner, Harriet. *The Dance of Deception.* HarperPerrenial. 1993.

Lerner, Harriet. *The Dance of Anger.* HarperPerrenial. 1987.

LeShan, Lawrence. *How to Meditate.* Bantam. 1974.

Levin, Kenneth. *Unconscious Fantasy in Psychotherapy.* Jason Aronson, Inc. 1993

Levoy, Gregg. *Callings: Finding and Following an Authentic Life.* Harmony. 1997.

Lifton, Robert Jay. *The Protean Self: Human Resilience in an Age of Fragmentation.* Basic. 1993.

Lindenfield, Gael. *Assert Yourself.* HarperPaperbacks. 1986.

Llewellyn, Grace. *The Teenage Liberation Handbook.* Element. 1997.

Loftus, Elizabeth, and Ketchum, Katherine. *Witness for the Defense: The Accused, The Eyewitness and the Expert Who Puts Memory On Trial.* St. Martin's Press. 1991.

Loftus, Elizabeth, and Ketchum, Katherine. *The Myth of Repressed Memory: False Memory and Allegations of Sexual Abuse.* St. Martin's Griffin. 1994.

Louden, Jennifer. *The Woman's Comfort Book: A Self-Nurturing Guide for Restoring Balance in Your Life.* HarperSanFransciso. 1992.

Madanes, Cloé, and Madanes, Claudio. *The Secret Meaning Of Money.* Jossey-Bass. 1994.

Madanes, Cloé. *Sex, Love, and Violence.* W.W. Norton. 1990.

Madanes, Cloé. *Behind the One-Way Mirror.* Jossey-Bass. 1984.

Maisel, Eric. *Deep Writing: 7 Principles that Bring Ideas to Life.* Jeremy P. Tarcher. 1999.

Maisel, Eric. *Fearless Creating.* Jeremy P. Tarcher. 1995.

Maisel, Eric. *A Life in the Arts.* Jeremy P. Tarcher. 1992.

Margulis, Lynn, and Sagan, Dorion. *Slanted Truths.* Copernicus. 1997.

Mariechild, Diane. *Mother Wit: A Guide to Healing & Psychic Development.* Crossing Press. 1981.

Maslow, Abraham H. *The Farther Reaches of Human Nature.* Viking/Esalen. 1971.

Maslow, Abraham H. *Toward a Psychology of Being*. Van Nostrand. 1962.

Maslow, Abraham H. *Religions, Values, And Peak-Experiences*. Viking Press. 1964.

Masson, Jeffrey Moussaieff. *The Assault on Truth: Freud's Suppression of the Seduction Theory*. HarperPerrenial. 1984.

Masson, Jeffrey Moussaieff. *My Father's Guru: A Journey Through Spirituality and Disillusion*. Addison-Wesley. 1993.

Masson, Jeffrey Moussaieff. *Final Analysis: The Making and Unmaking of a Psychoanalyst*. Addison-Wesley Publishing, Inc. 1990.

Masson, Jeffrey Moussaieff. *Against Therapy*. Common Courage Press. 1988.

Masters, Robert, and Houston, Jean. *Mind Games: The Guide to Inner Space*. Barnes & Noble. 1972.

Mazza, Joan. *Dreaming Your Real Self: A Personal Approach to Dream Interpretation*. Perigee/PenguinPutnam. 1998.

Mazza, Joan. *Dream Back Your Life: Transforming Dream Messages into Life Action—A Practical Guide to Dreams, Daydreams, and Fantasies*. Perigee/PenguinPutnam. 2000.

Mazza, Joan. *From Dreams to Self-Discovery*. Writer's Digest. 2000.

Mellody, Pia. *Facing Codependence*. HarperSanFrancisco. 1989.

Metzger, Deena. *Writing for Your Life*. HarperSanFrancisco. 1992.

Miller, Alice. *Banished Knowledge: Facing Childhood Injuries.* Anchor/Doubleday. 1988.

Miller, Alice. *Thou Shalt Not Be Aware: Society's Betrayal of the Child.* Meridian/Penguin. 1986.

Miller, Alice. *For Your Own Good: Hidden Cruelty in Child-Rearing and the Roots of Violence.* Noonday Press. 1983.

Miller, Alice. *Breaking Down the Wall of Silence: The Liberating Experience of Facing Painful Truth.* Meridian/Penguin. 1993.

Miller, Jean Baker. *Toward a New Psychology of Women.* Beacon Press. 1986.

Mithers, Carol Lynn. *Therapy Gone Mad: The True Story of Hundreds of Patients and a Generation Betrayed.* Addison-Wesley. 1994.

Money, John. *Lovemaps.* Irvington/Prometheus. 1986.

Money, John. *Gay, Straight and In-Between: The Sexology of Erotic Orientation.* Oxford University Press. 1988.

Money, John, and Lamacz, Margaret. *Vandalized Lovemaps: Paraphilic Outcome of Seven Cases in Pediatric Sexology.* Prometheus. 1989.

Moore, Thomas. *The Re-Enchantment of Everyday Life.* HarperPerrenial. 1997.

Moore, Thomas. *Care Of The Soul: Guide for Cultivating Depth and Sacredness in Everyday Life.* HarperCollins. 1992.

Moran, Jim. *Some Things Never Change*. Great Quotations, Inc. 1996.

Moreno, J.L. *The Essential Moreno*. Springer. 1987.

Morris, Desmond. *Intimate Behavior: A Zoologist's Classic Study of Intimate Behavior*. Kodansha International. 1995.

Moustakas, Clark. *Existential Psychotherapy and the Interpretation of Dreams*. Jason Aronson. 1994.

Muller, Wayne. *Legacy Of The Heart: The Spiritual Advantages of a Painful Childhood*. Fireside/Simon & Schuster. 1992.

Muller, Wayne. *How, Then, Shall We Live? Four Simple Questions That Reveal The Beauty and Meaning of our Lives*. Bantam. 1996.

Myss, Caroline. *Anatomy of the Spirit*. Three Rivers Press. 1996.

Nathan, Debbie, and Snedeker, Michael. *Satan's Silence: Ritual Abuse and the Making of a Modern American Witch-Hunt*. BasicBooks. 1995

Nelson, John E., and Nelson, Andrea, editors. *Sacred Sorrows: Embracing and Transforming Depression*. Jeremy P. Tarcher/Putnam. 1996.

Norden, Michael J. *Beyond Prozac*. ReganBooks. 1995.

O'Hanlon, William, and Weiner-Davis, Michele. *In Search of Solutions: A New Direction in Psychotherapy*. W.W. Norton. 1989.

Ofshe, Richard and Watters, Ethan. *Making Monsters: False Memories, Psychotherapy, And Sexual Hysteria.* Charles Scribner's Sons. 1994.

Ornstein, Robert, and Sobel, David. *Healthy Pleasures.* Addison-Wesley Publishing. 1989.

Orsborn, Carol. *The Art of Resilience.* Three Rivers Press/Crown. 1997.

Palmer, Helen, editor. *Inner Knowing: Consciousness, Creativity, Insight, Intuition.* Jeremy P. Tarcher. 1998.

Pearson, Carol S. *Awakening the Heroes Within.* HarperSanFrancisco. 1991.

Pearson, Carol S. *The Hero Within: Six Archetypes We Live By.* HarperSanFrancisco. 1986.

Peck, M. Scott. *The Road Less Traveled: A New Psychology of Love, Traditional Values and Spiritual Growth.* Touchstone/Simon & Schuster. 1978.

Peele, Stanton, *Diseasing of America.* Lexington. 1995.

Pendergrast, Mark. *Victims of Memory: Sex Abuse Accusations and Shattered Lives.* Upper Access. 1996.

Perls, Frederick S. *Gestalt Therapy Verbatim.* Bantam. 1969.

Perry, Susan K. *Playing Smart: A Parent's Guide to Enriching, Offbeat Learning* Free Spirit. 1990.

Perry, Susan K. *Writing in Flow: Keys to Enhanced Creativity.* Writer's Digest. 1999.

Peterson, Marilyn R. *At Personal Risk: Boundary Violations in Professional-Client Relationships.* W.W. Norton. 1992.

Phelps, Stanlee, and Austin, Nancy. *The Assertive Woman.* Impact. 1997.

Pike, Diane Kennedy. *Life as a Waking Dream.* Riverhead Books. 1997.

Pittman, Frank. *Grow Up! How Taking Responsibility Can Make You a Happy Adult.* St. Martin's Griffin. 1998.

Polster, Erving & Miriam. *Gestalt Therapy Integrated.* Vintage. 1973.

Progoff, Ira. *At A Journal Workshop: Writing To Access The Power Of The Unconscious And Evoke Creative Ability.* Jeremy P. Tarcher. 1975.

Pryor, Karen. *Don't Shoot The Dog! The New Art Of Teaching And Training.* Bantam. 1984.

Rainer, Tristine. *The New Diary: How To Use A Journal For Self-Guidance And Expanded Creativity.* Jeremy P. Tarcher. 1978.

Ratey, John J., and Johnson, Catherine. *Shadow Syndromes: The Mild Forms of Major Mental Disorders that Sabotage Us.* Bantam. 1997.

Ratey, John J., and Hallowell, Edward M. *Driven to Distraction: Recognizing and Coping with Attention Deficit Disorder.* Touchstone/Simon & Schuster. 1994.

Reynolds, David K. *Thirsty, Swimming In The Lake.* Quill. 1991.

Reynolds, David K. *Playing Ball on Running Water.* Quill. 1984.

Robbins, Anthony. *Notes From A Friend: A Quick and Simple Guide to Taking Charge of Your Life.* Simon & Schuster. 1995.

Robbins, Anthony. *Unlimited Power.* Fawcett Columbine. 1986.

Robertiello, Richard C., Schoenewolf, G. *101 Common Therapeutic Blunders.* Jason Aronson. 1987.

Robertson, Joel, with Tom Monte. *Natural Prozac: Learning To Release Your Body's Own Anti-Depressants.* HarperSanFrancisco. 1997

Rogers, Carl. *A Way of Being.* Houghton Mifflin Co. 1980.

Rogers, Carl. *On Becoming a Person.* Houghton Mifflin Co. 1961.

Rosenberg, Marshall B. *Nonviolent Communication: A Language of Compassion.* PuddleDancer Press. 1999.

Rubin, Lillian. *The Transcendent Child: Tales of Triumph over the Past.* BasicBooks. 1996.

Ruchlis, Hy, and Oddo, Sandra. *Critical Thinking: A Practical Introduction.* Prometheus. 1990.

Rusk, Tom, and Miller, D. Patrick. *Instead Of Therapy: Help Yourself Change & Change The Help You're Getting.* Hay House. 1991.

Sagan, Carl. *The Demon-Haunted World: Science as a Candle in the Dark.* Random House. 1995.

Sager, Clifford J., and Hunt, Bernice. *Intimate Partners: Hidden Patterns in Love Relationships.* McGraw-Hill. 1979.

Sakheim, David K., and Devine, Susan E. *Out of Darkness: Exploring Satanism & Ritual Abuse*. Lexington Books. 1992.

Sanders, Pete A. *Access Our Brain's Joy Center*. Free Soul. 1996.

Sartre, Jean-Paul. *Existential Psychoanalysis* Regnery Publishing 1981

Schacter, Daniel L. *Searching for Memory: The Brain, the Mind, and the Past*. BasicBooks. 1996.

Schiffer, Fredric. *Of Two Minds: The Revolutionary Science of Dual-Brain Psychology*. The Free Press. 1998.

Schwartz, Jeffrey M. *Brain Lock*. ReganBooks. 1996.

Scott, Gini Graham. *Making Ethical Choices: Resolving Ethical Dilemmas*. Paragon House. 1998.

Seabury, David. *The Art of Selfishness*. Cornerstone Library. 1937.

Seligman, Martin. *Learned Optimism: How to Change Your Mind and Your Life*. Pocket. 1990.

Seligman, Martin. *What You Can Change...And What You Can't: Learning to Accept Who You Are*. Fawcett Columbine. 1993.

Shapiro, Francine, and Forrest, Margot Silk. *EMDR: The Breakthrough Therapy For Overcoming Anxiety, Stress, And Trauma*. Basic Books. 1997.

Sher, Barbara, with Annie Gottlieb. *Wishcraft: How To Get What You Really Want*. Ballantine. 1979.

Sher, Barbara, with Annie Gottlieb. *Live the Life You Love.* Delacorte. 1996.

Sher, Barbara, with Barbara Smith. *I Could Do Anything, If I Only Knew What It Was.* Dell. 1994.

Showalter, Elaine. *Hystories: Hysterical Epidemics and Modern Media.* Columbia University Press. 1997.

Siebert, Al. *Peaking Out: How My Mind Broke Free from the Delusions in Psychiatry.* Practical Psychology Press. 1995.

Siebert, Al. *The Survivor Personality: Why Some People are Stronger, Smarter, and More Skillful at Handling Life's Difficulties.* Perigee. 1996.

Simon, Sidney B., and Howe, Leland. *Values Clarification.* Warner. 1995.

Simon, Sidney B., and Howard Kirschenbaum, Howard.

Sinetar, Marsha. *Do What You Love, The Money Will Follow.* Dell. 1987.

Singer, Margaret Thaler, and Lalich, Janja. *Cults in Our Midst: The Hidden Menace in Our Everyday Lives.* Jossey-Bass Publishers. 1995.

Singer, Margaret Thaler, and Lalich, Janja. *"Crazy" Thrapies.* Jossey-Bass Publishers. 1996.

Smith, Hyrum W. *The 10 Natural Laws Of Successful Time And Life Management.* Warner. 1994.

Smith, Ann W. *Overcoming Perfectionism.* Health Communications. 1990.

Smith, Manuel J. *When I Say No, I Feel Guilty.* Bantam. 1975.

St. James, Elaine. *Simplify Your Life.* Hyperion. 1996.

Stearns, Ann Kaiser, and Lamplugh, Rick. *Living Through Job Loss.* Simon & Schuster. 1995.

Stein, Ronald H. *Ethical Issues in Counseling.* Prometheus. 1990.

Steinberg, David. *The Erotic Impulse: Honoring the Sensual Self.* Jeremy P. Tarcher. 1992.

Sternberg, Patricia, and Garcia, Antonina. *Sociodrama: Who's in Your Shoes?* Praeger. 1994.

Storr, Anthony. *Solitude: A Return to the Self.* Ballantine. 1988.

Sykes, Charles J. *A Nation of Victims: The Decay of the American Character.* St. Martin's. 1992.

Szasz, Thomas S. *The Myth of Mental Illness.* Dell Publishing. 1961.

Talmon, Moshe. *Single Session Therapy.* Jossey-Bass Publishers. 1990.

Tart, Charles T. *Waking Up: Overcoming the Obstacles to Human Potential.* Shambala. 1987.

Tart, Charles T. *Living the Mindful Life.* Shambala. 1994.

Tart, Charles T., editor. *Altered States of Consciousness.* Doubleday Anchor. 1969.

Tavris, Carol, and Wade, Carol. *Psychology in Perspective, 2nd ed.* Addison Wesley. 1997.

Tavris, Carol. *Anger: The Misunderstood Emotion.*
Touchstone/Simon & Schuster. 1989.

Tavris, Carol. *The Mismeasure of Woman.* Simon & Schuster. 1992.

Terr, Lenore. *Unchained Memories: True Stories of Traumatic Memories Lost and Found.* BasicBooks. 1994.

Tessina, Tina. *The Real Thirteenth Step.* Jeremy Tarcher. 1991.

Torrey, E. Fuller. *Mind Game: Witchdoctors and Psychiatrists.* Jason Aronson. 1983.

Vanzant, Iyanla. *In the Meantime.* Simon & Schuster. 1998.

Ventura, Michael. *Shadow Dancing in the USA.* Jeremy Tarcher. 1985.

Ventura, Michael. *Letters At 3 AM: Reports on Endarkenment.* Spring Publications. 1993.

Victor, Jeffrey S. *Satanic Panic: The Creation of a Contemporary Legend.* Open Court Press. 1993.

Viscott, David. *Emotional Resilience: Simple Truths for Dealing with the Unfinished Business of Your Past.* Harmony. 1996.

Von Franz, Marie-Louise. *Psychotherapy.* Shambala.1993.

Walsh, Roger, & Vaughan, F. (editors) *Paths Beyond Ego: The Transpersonal Vision.* Jeremy P. Tarcher/Putnam. 1993.

Walter, John. L., and Peller, Jane E. *Becoming Solution-Focused in Brief Therapy.* Brunner/Mazel. 1992.

Weinberg, George. *The Heart of Psychotherapy: A Journey into the Mind and Office of the Psychotherapist at Work.* St. Martin's. 1984.

Weiner-Davis, Michele. *Divorce Busting.* Fireside/Simon & Schuster. 1992.

Weiner-Davis, Michele. *Change Your Life and Everyone In It.* Fireside/Simon & Schuster. 1995.

Weissman, Steve & Rosemary. *Meditation, Compassion, & Lovingkindness: An Approach to Vipassana Meditation.* Samuel Weiser, Inc. 1996.

Welwood, John, editor. *Ordinary Magic: Everyday Life as Spiritual Path.* Shambala. 1992.

Wheelis, Allen. *How People Change.* Perrenial/Harper & Row. 1973.

White, Michael, and Epston, David. *Narrative Means to Therapeutic Ends.* W.W. Norton. 1990.

Whitfield, Charles L. *Boundaries and Relationships.* Health Communications, Inc. 1993.

Whitfield, Charles L. *Memory and Abuse: Remembering and Healing the Effects of Trauma.* Health Communications, Inc. 1995.

Whitmont, Edward C., and Perera, Sylvia Brinton. *Dreams: A Portal to the Source.* Routledge. 1989.

Whitmyer, Claude, editor. *In The Company Of Others: Making Community In The Modern World.* Jeremy P. Tarcher. 1993.

Witcher, Barbara Johnson. *Create the Job You Love*. Prima Publishing. 1997.

Wolin, Steven J., and Wolin, Sybil. *The Resilient Self: How Survivors of Troubled Families Rive Above Adversity*. Villard Books. 1993.

Wolinsky, Stephen. with Margaret O. Ryan. *Trances People Live: Healing Approaches in Quantum Psychology*. The Bramble Company. 1991.

Wood, Garth. *The Myth of Neurosis*. Harper & Row. 1983.

Wycoff, Joyce. *Mindmapping: Your Personal Guide to Exploring Creativity and Problem-Solving*. Berkley. 1991.

Yalom, Irvin. The Yalom Reader. BasicBooks. 1998.

Yalom, Irvin. *The Theory and Practice of Group Psychotherapy*. BasicBooks. 1975.

Yapko, Michael D. *Suggestions of Abuse: True and False Memories of Childhood Sexual Trauma*. Simon & Schuster. 1994.

Yapko, Michael D. *Breaking the Patterns of Depression*. Main Street Books/Doubleday. 1997.

Young, Allan. *The Harmony of Illusions: Inventing Post-Traumatic Stress Disorder*. Princeton University Press. 1995.

Zilbergeld, Bernie. *The New Male Sexuality*. Bantam. 1992.

Zweig, Connie, & Abrams, Jeremiah, editors. *Meeting The Shadow: The Hidden Power of the Dark Side of Human Nature*. Jeremy P. Tarcher. 1991.

Zweig, Connie. Wolf, Steve. *Romancing the Shadow: Illuminating the Dark Side of the Soul.* Ballantine. 1997.

Books by Joan Mazza

Dreaming Your Real Self: A Personal Approach to Dream Interpretation (Perigee/Penguin Putnam, July 1998)

Who's Crazy, Anyway?—Everything You Always Wanted to Know about the Risks and Benefits of Psychotherapy, But Didn't Want to Have to Pay a Therapist to Find Out (iUniverse.com, April 2000)

Dream Back Your Life: Transforming Dream Messages into Life Action—A Practical Guide to Dreams, Daydreams, and Fantasies (Perigee/PenguinPutnam, July 2000)

From Dreams to Self-Discovery (Walking Stick Press/Writer's Digest Books, November 2000)

What Ticks Me Off (Walking Stick Press/Writer's Digest Books, February 2001)

Journaling Your Sexual Self (Walking Stick Press/Writer's Digest Books, April, 2001)

Joan Mazza is an author, speaker and licensed mental health counselor living in South Florida. She has appeared on radio and television as a dream specialist. She also teaches classes for continuing education to medical professionals and offers personal growth workshops to corporations and the public.

Joan Mazza
PO Box 70301
Fort Lauderdale, FL 33307-0301
(954) 564-6621 ¨ fax (954) 564-0001
joanm@aksi.net
http://www.joanmazza.com